Behind The Lens:
of Anthony M Mata

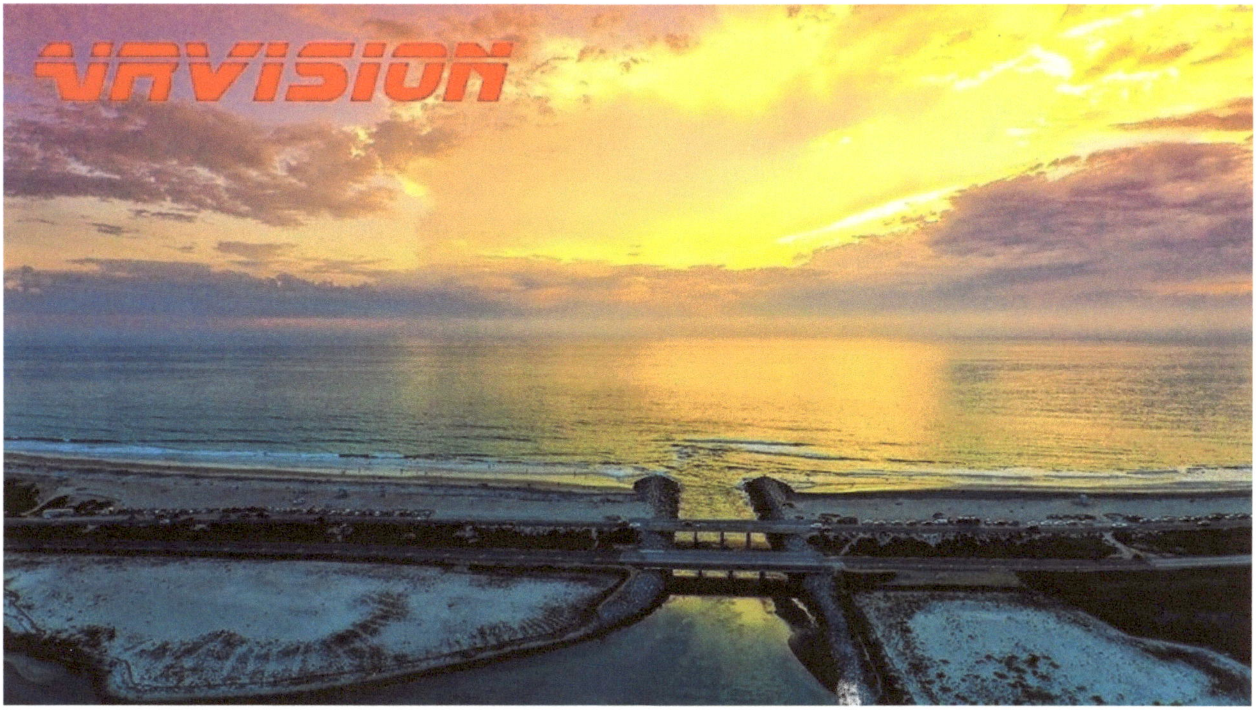

by

Bradley Zink

Copyright © 2017 Bradley Zink

All rights reserved.

ISBN: **1977881610**
ISBN-13: **978-1977881618**

DEDICATION

Music and Art is a crucial and integral part of our children's education and future.
I would like to dedicate this book to ALL of the children who strive and desire to learn the "arts", and who work and develop to become our Future leading Artists. I also dedicate this book to incredible photographers like Anthony Mata, who help inspire through their work, the "future" generations of photographic "artists".

"Let your Passion be your Guide"

ACKNOWLEDGMENTS

I would like to thank Anthony Mata, for offering to share his magnificent collection of photography with me.

Your unique perspective of our beautiful Carlsbad, with use of drone photography, helps capture the essence of "everyday life" here, with a rarely seen "bird's-eye view".

Thank you for all you do, for without your help, this book would not have been possible.

The Photographer

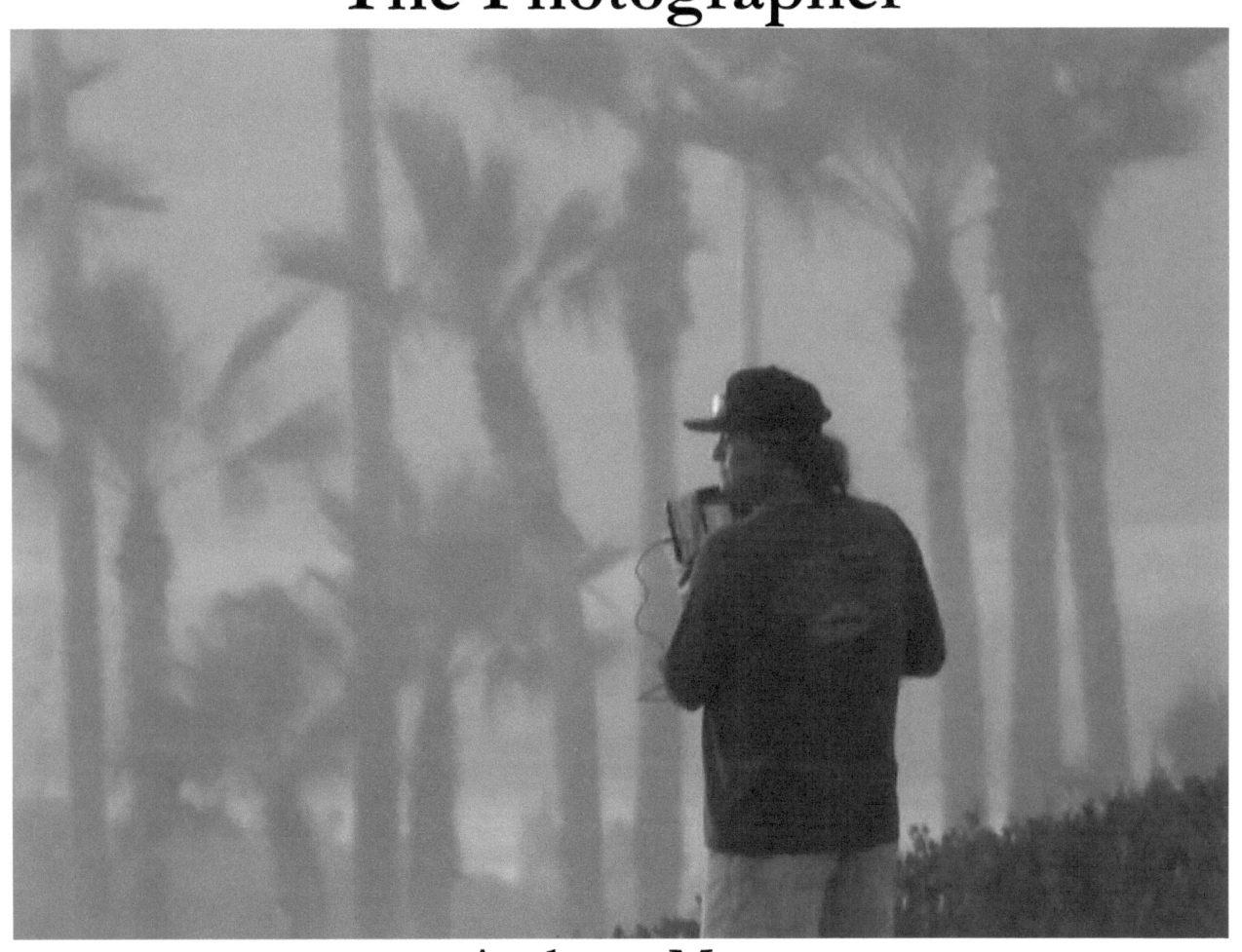

Anthony Mata

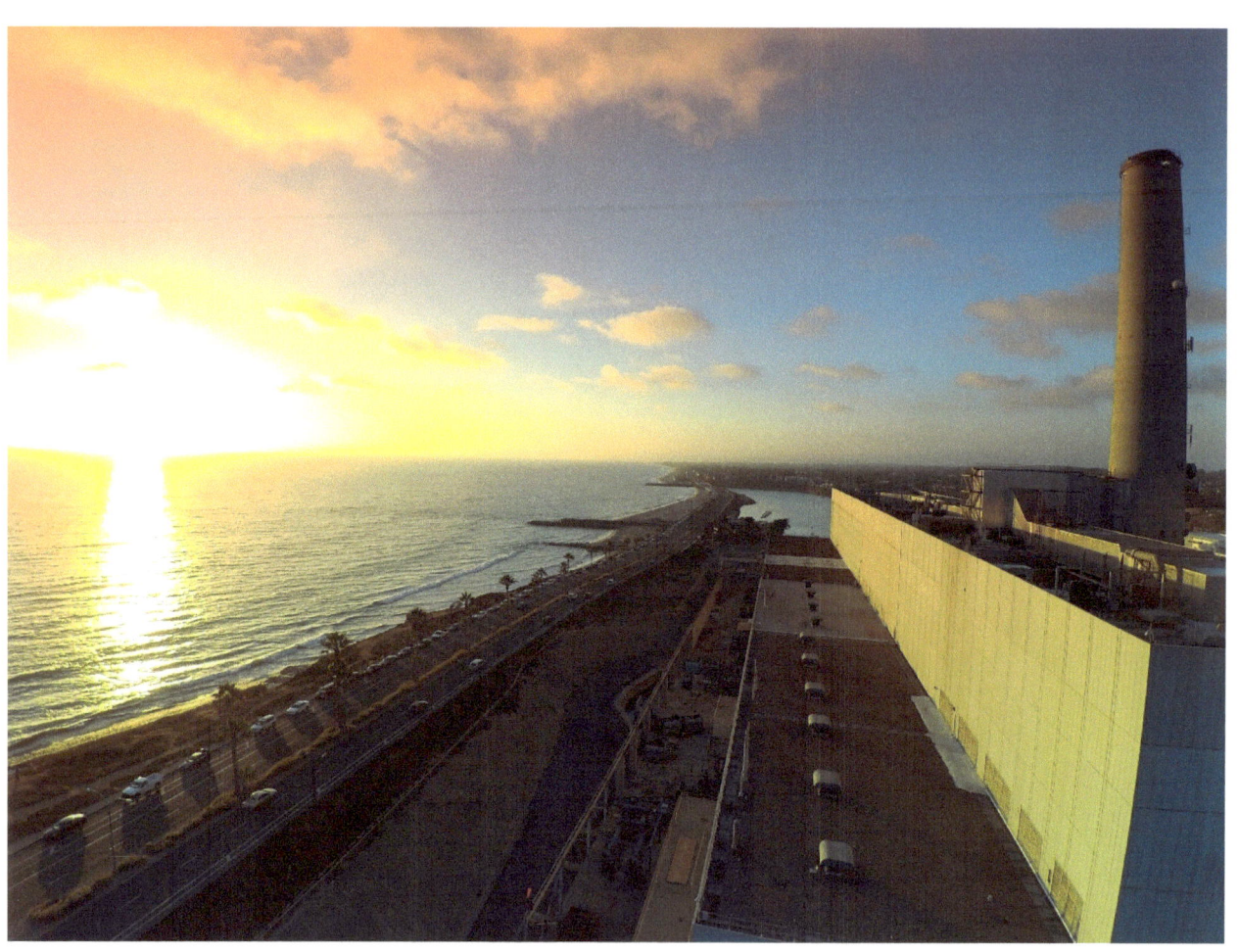

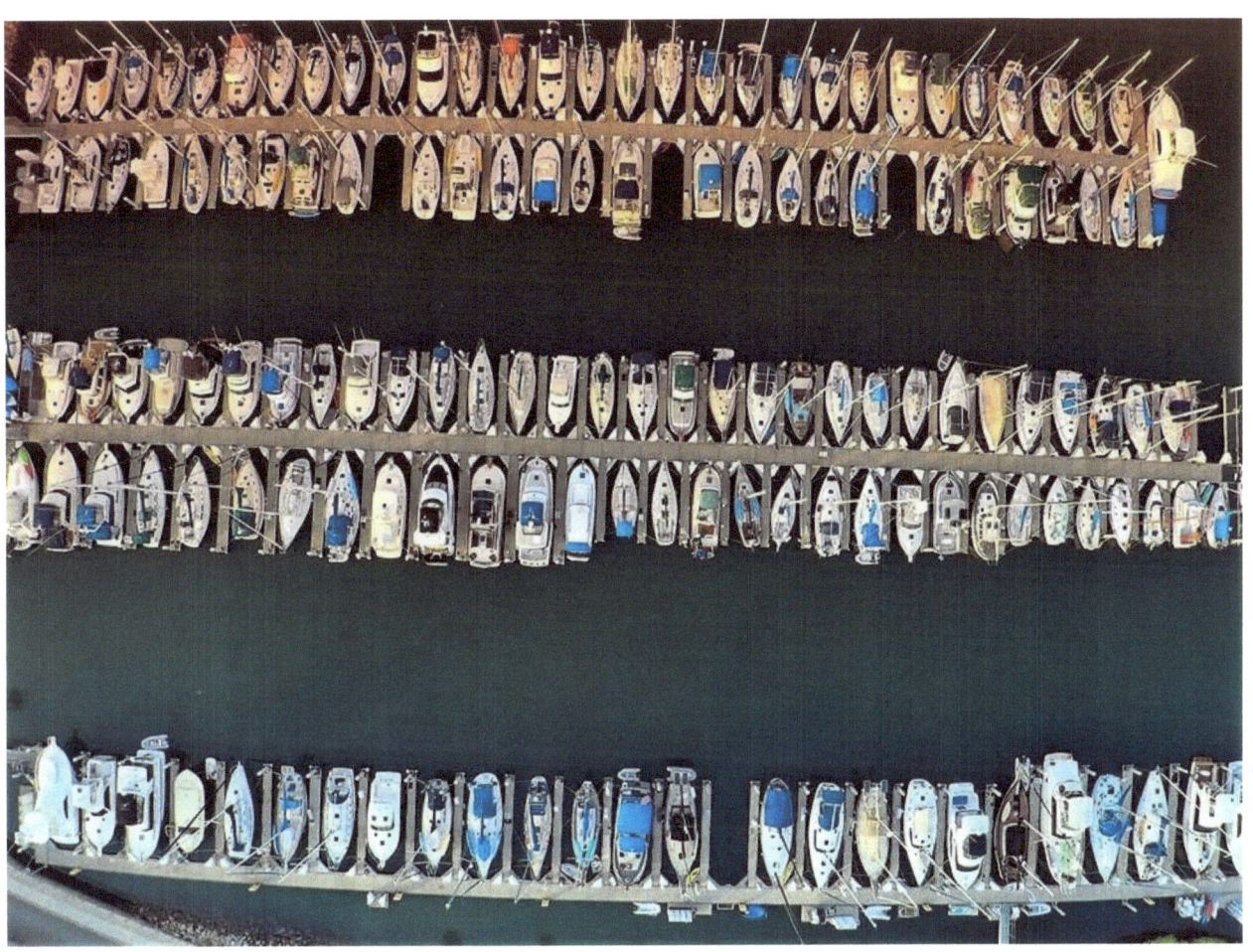

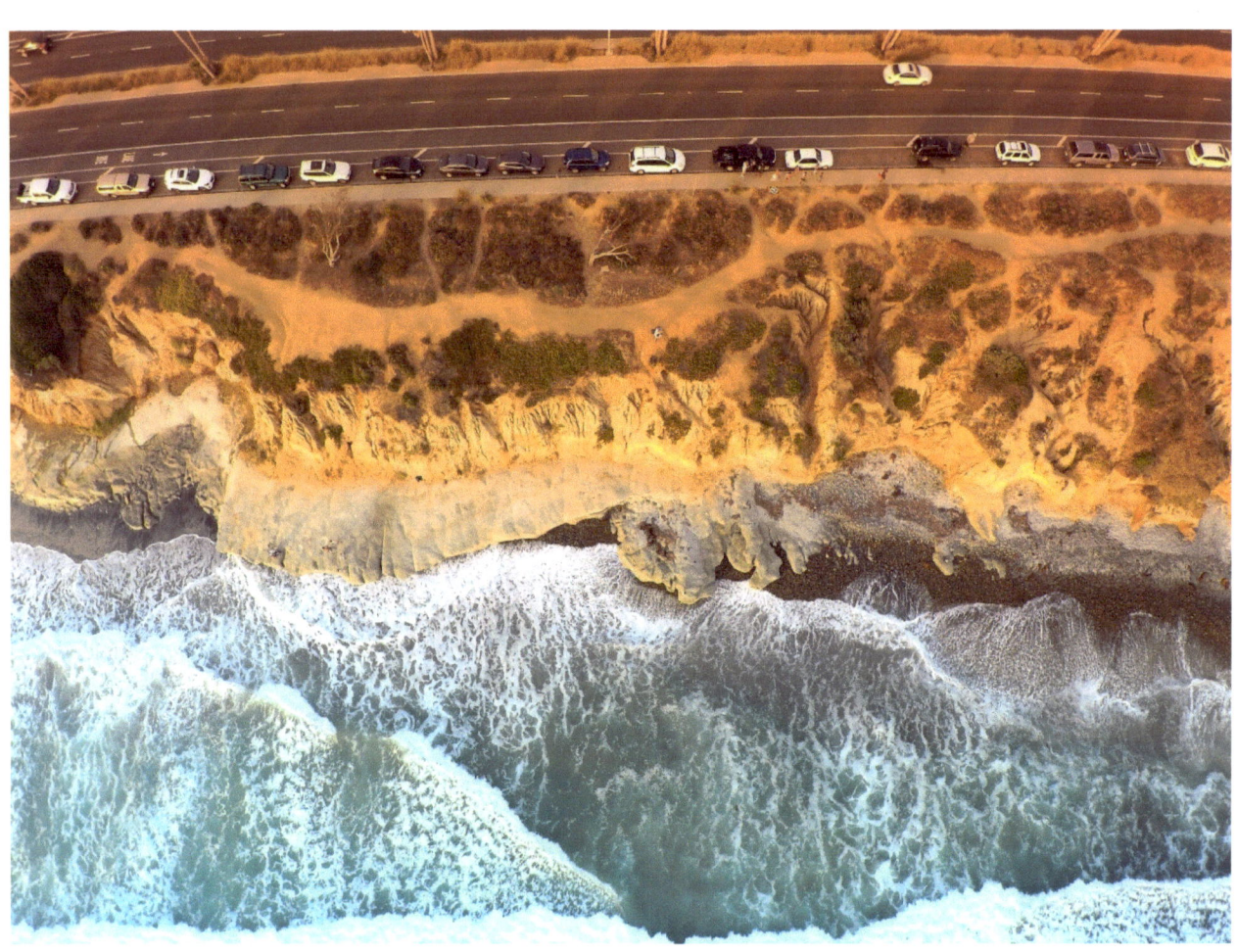

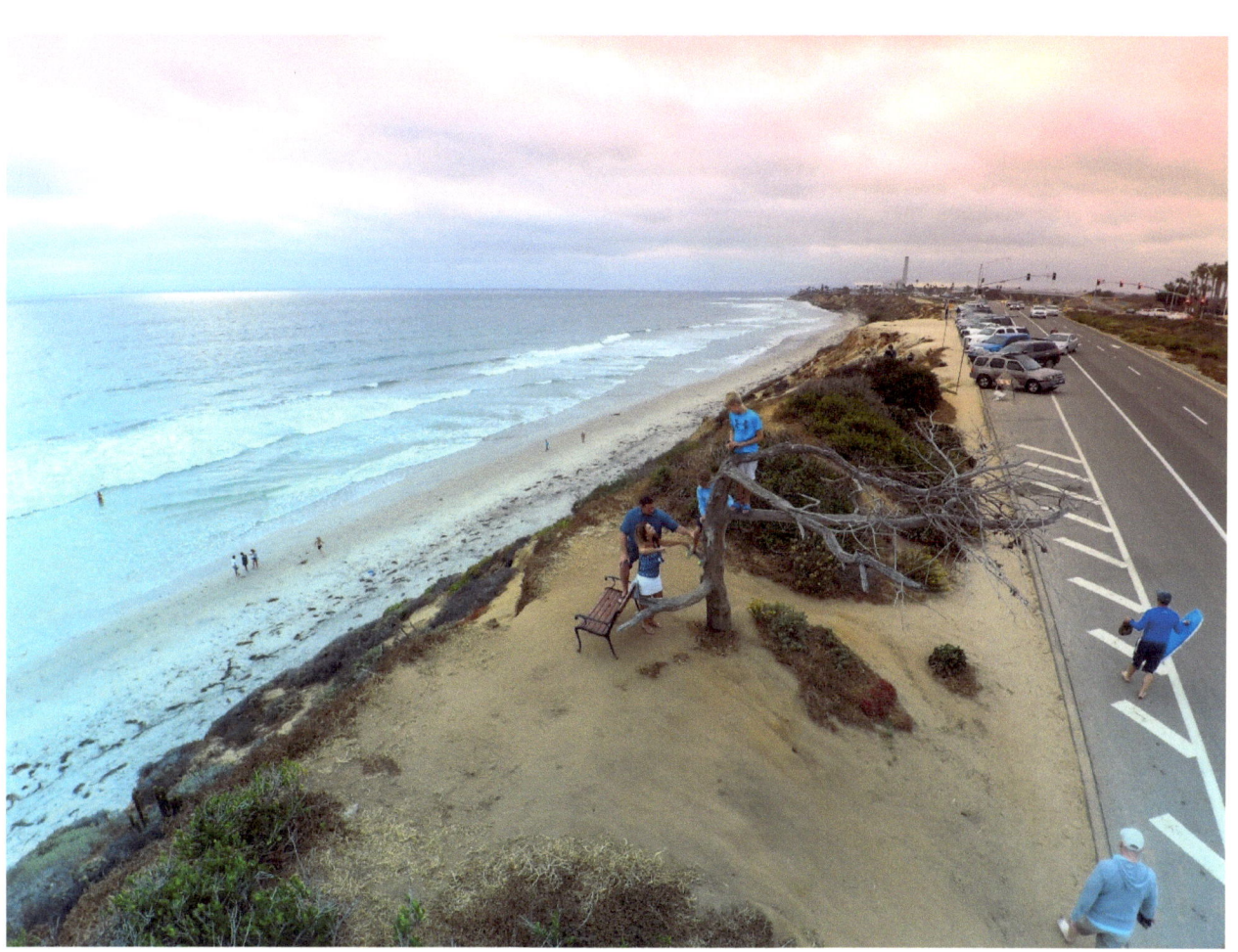

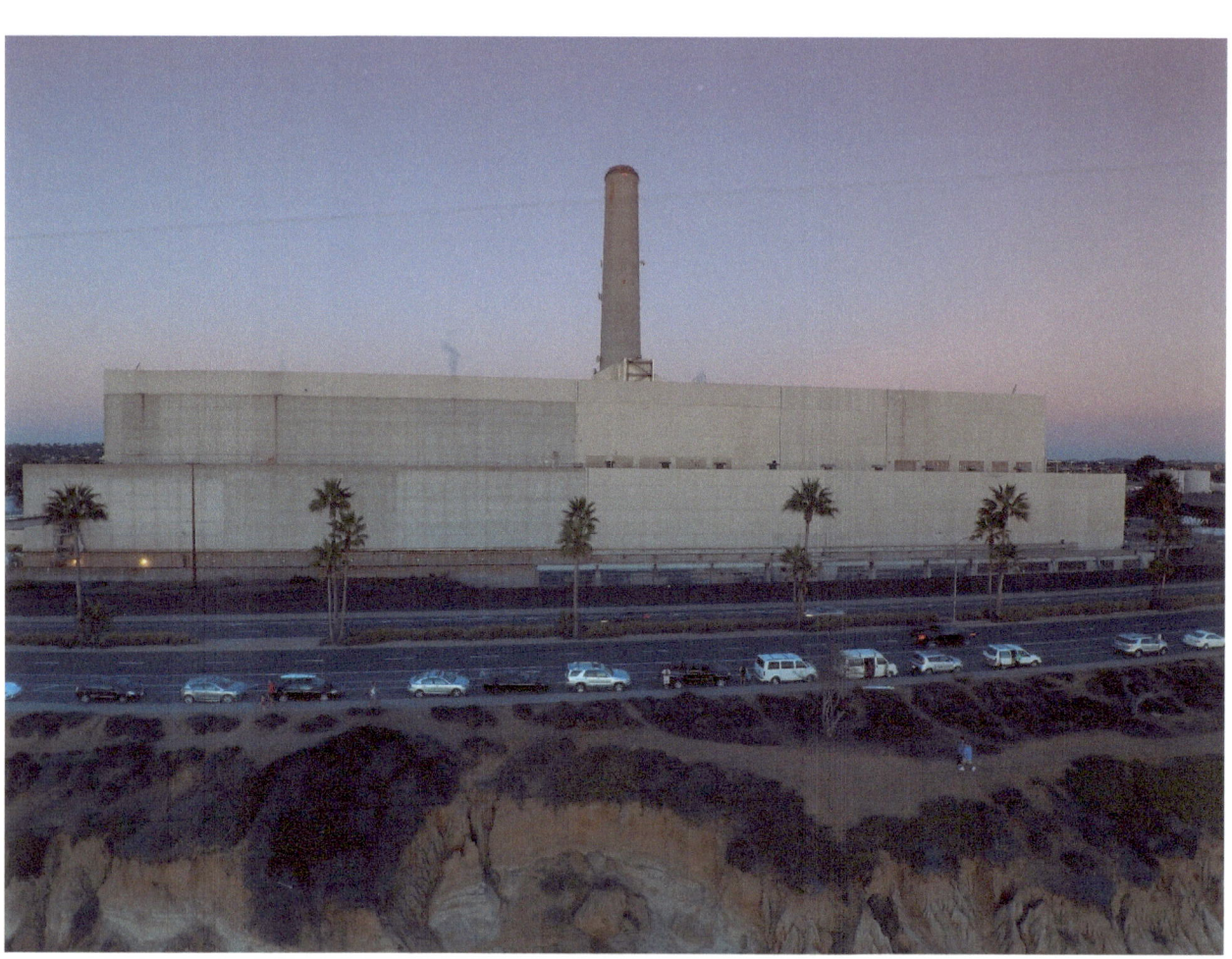

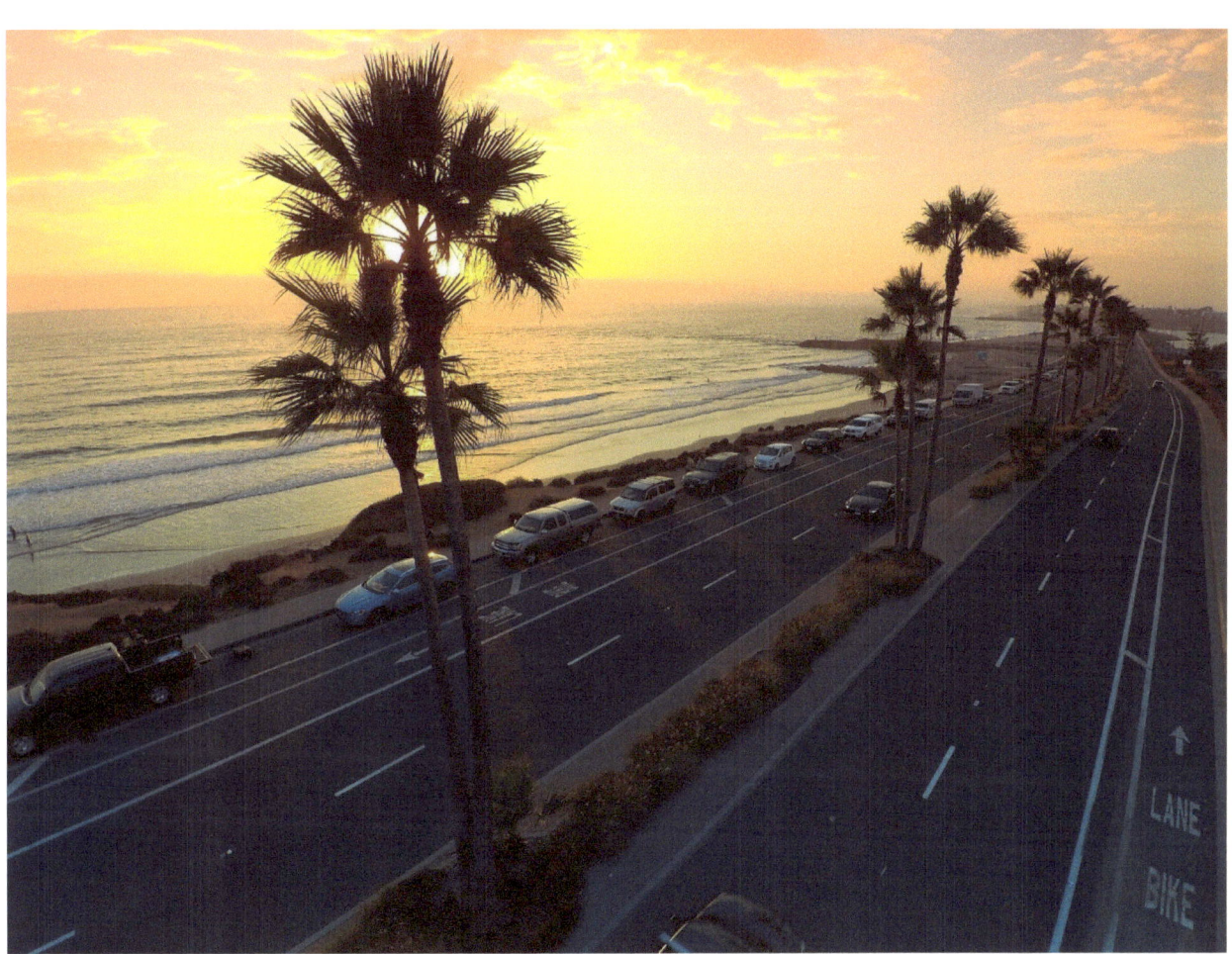

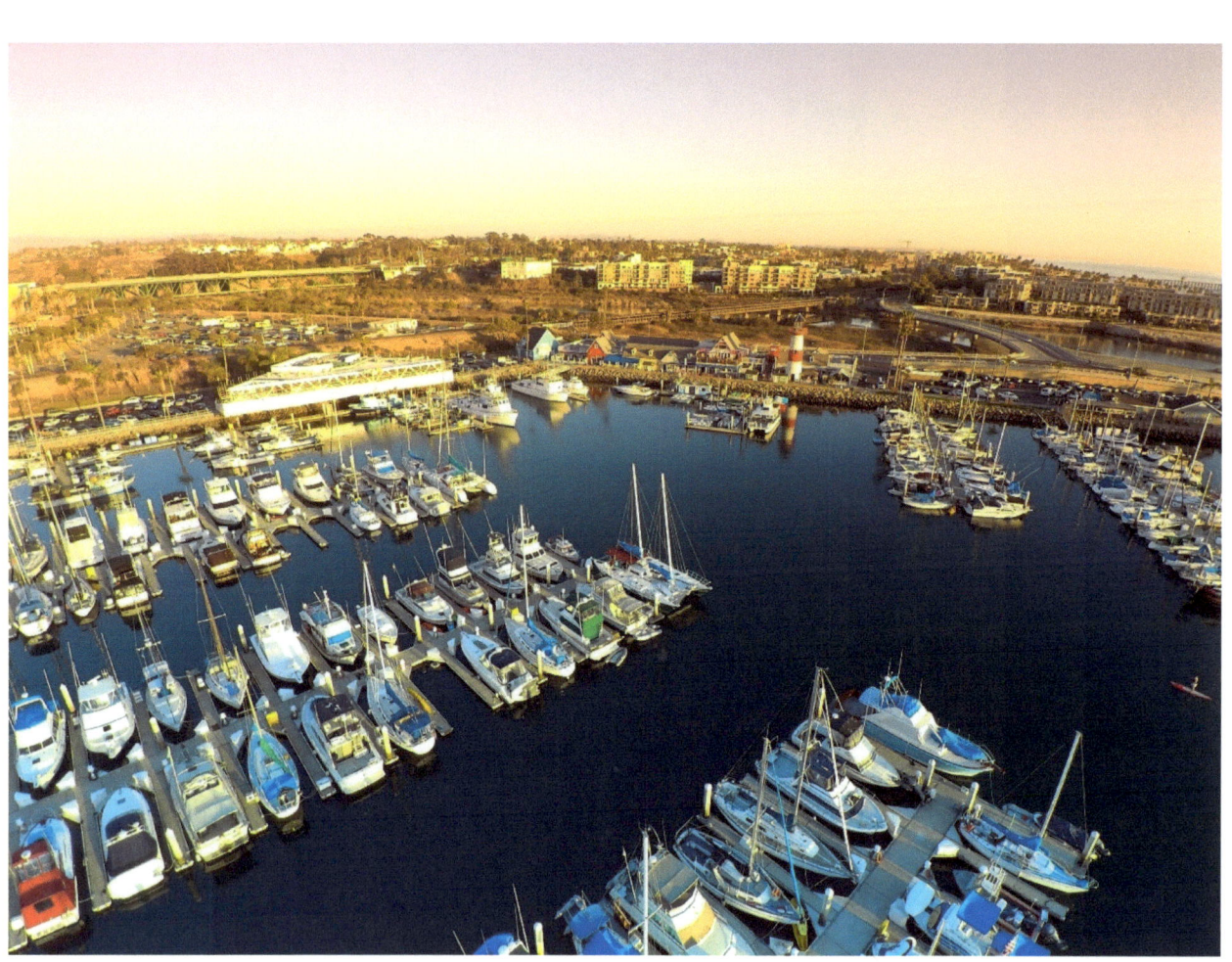

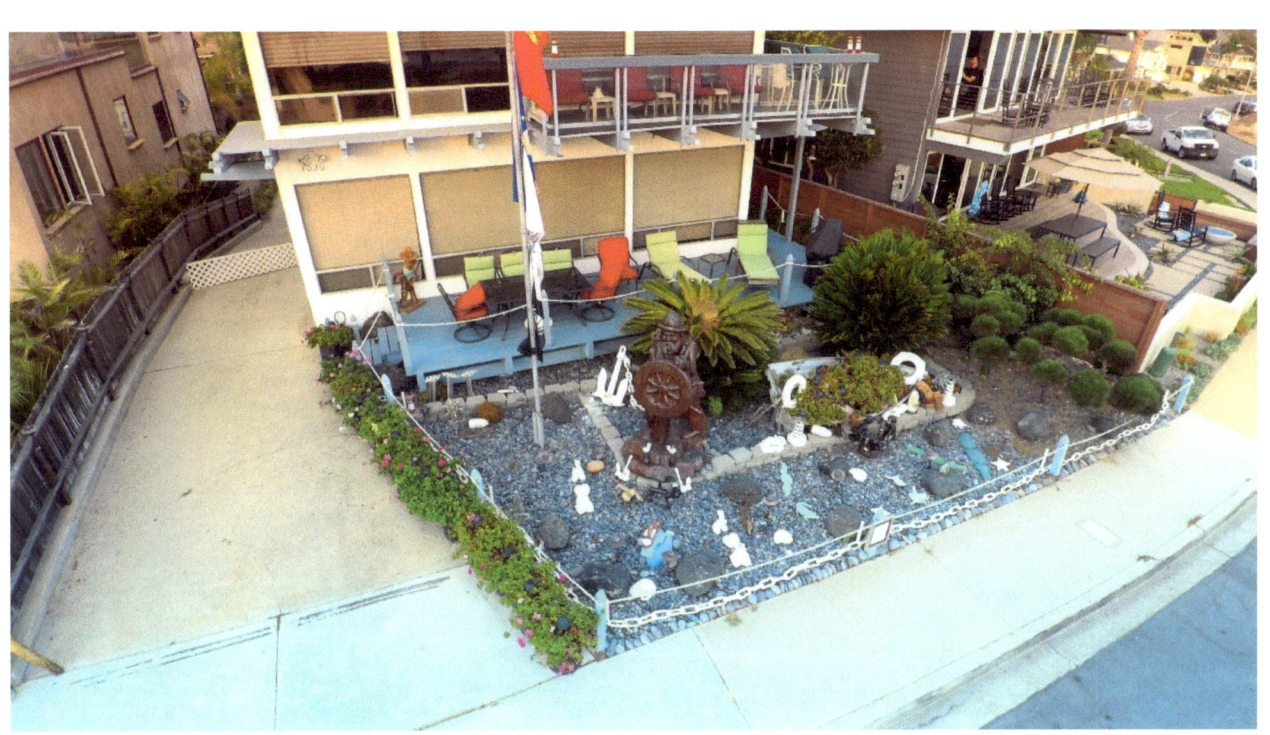

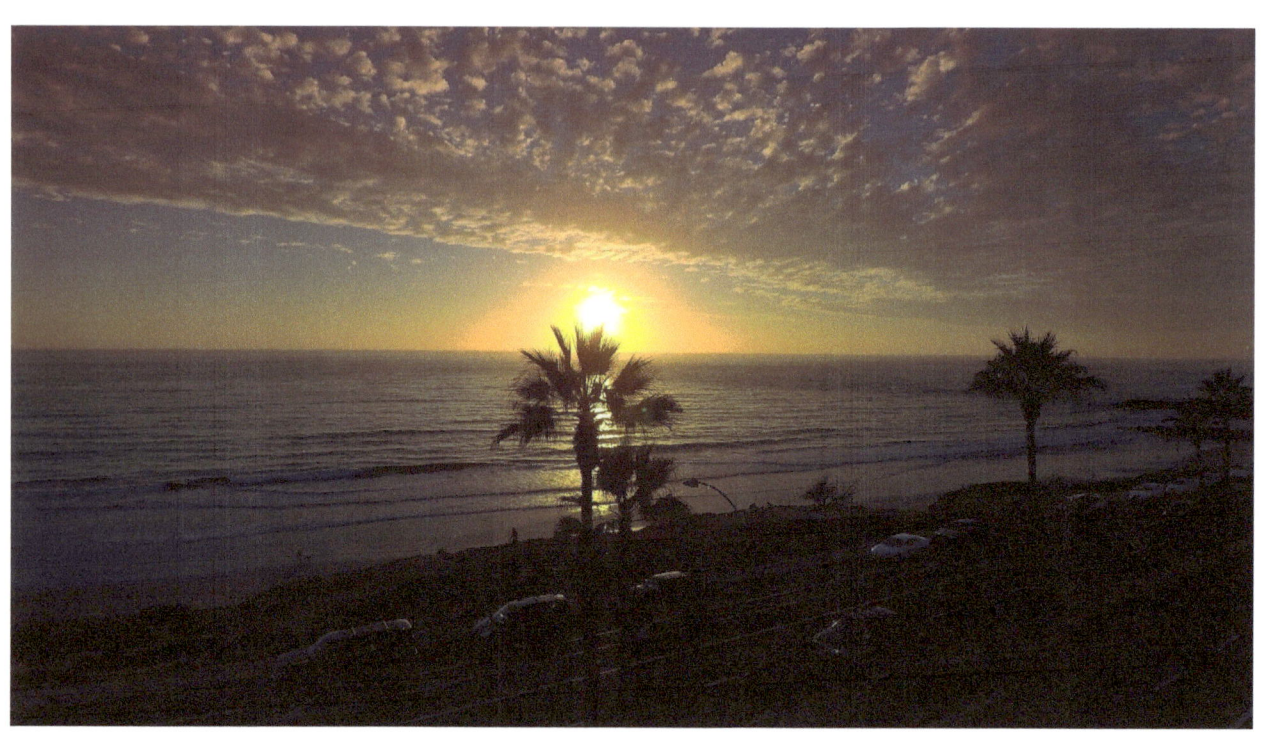

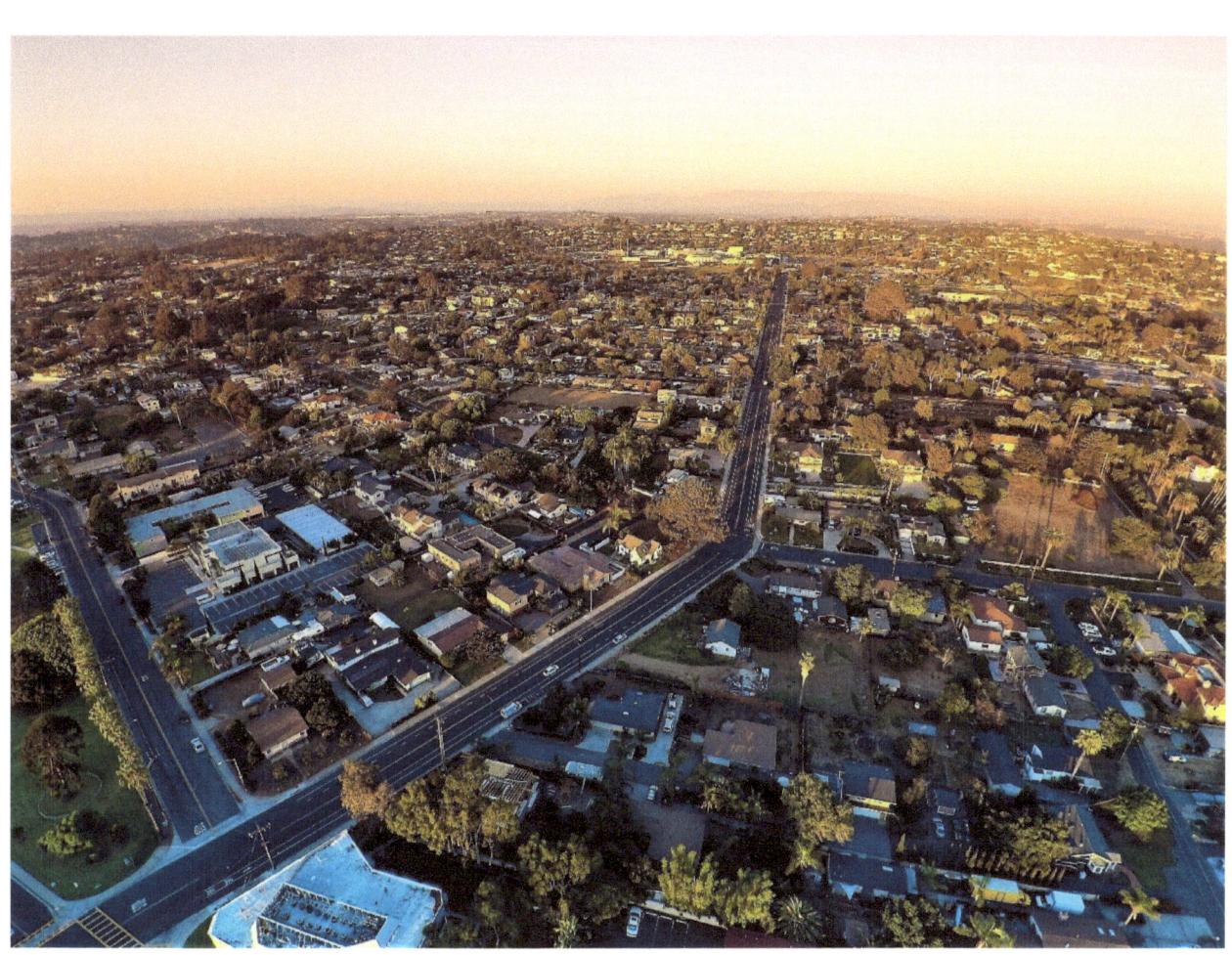

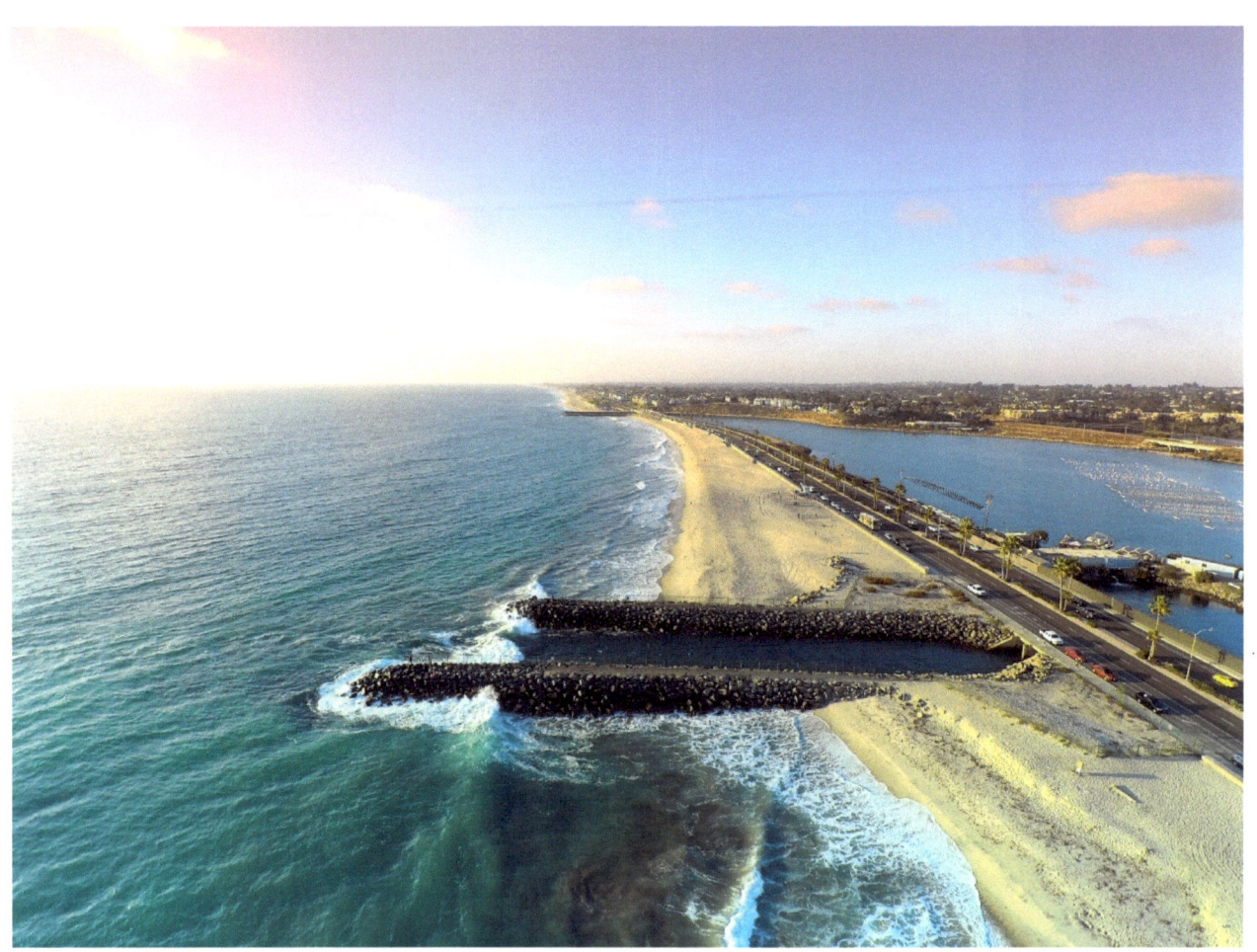

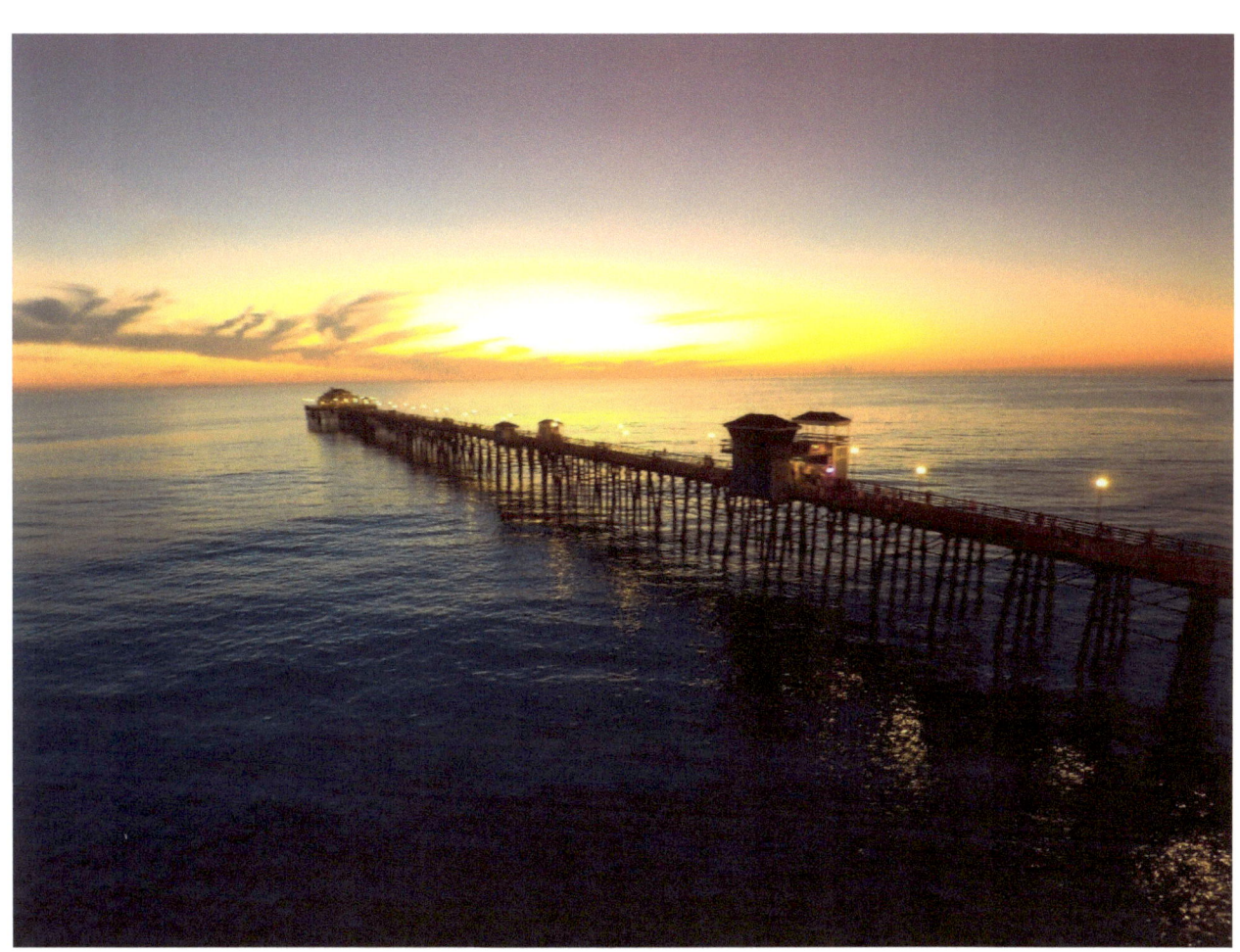

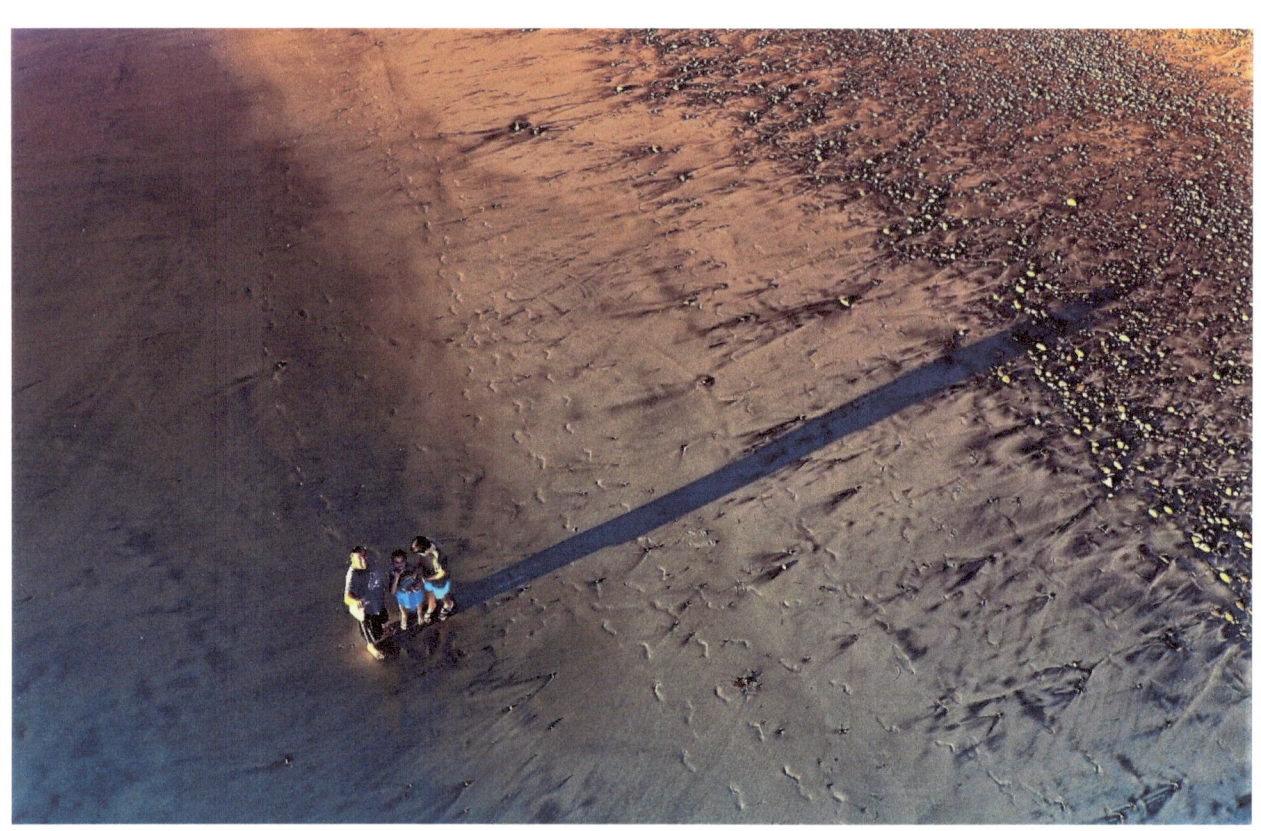

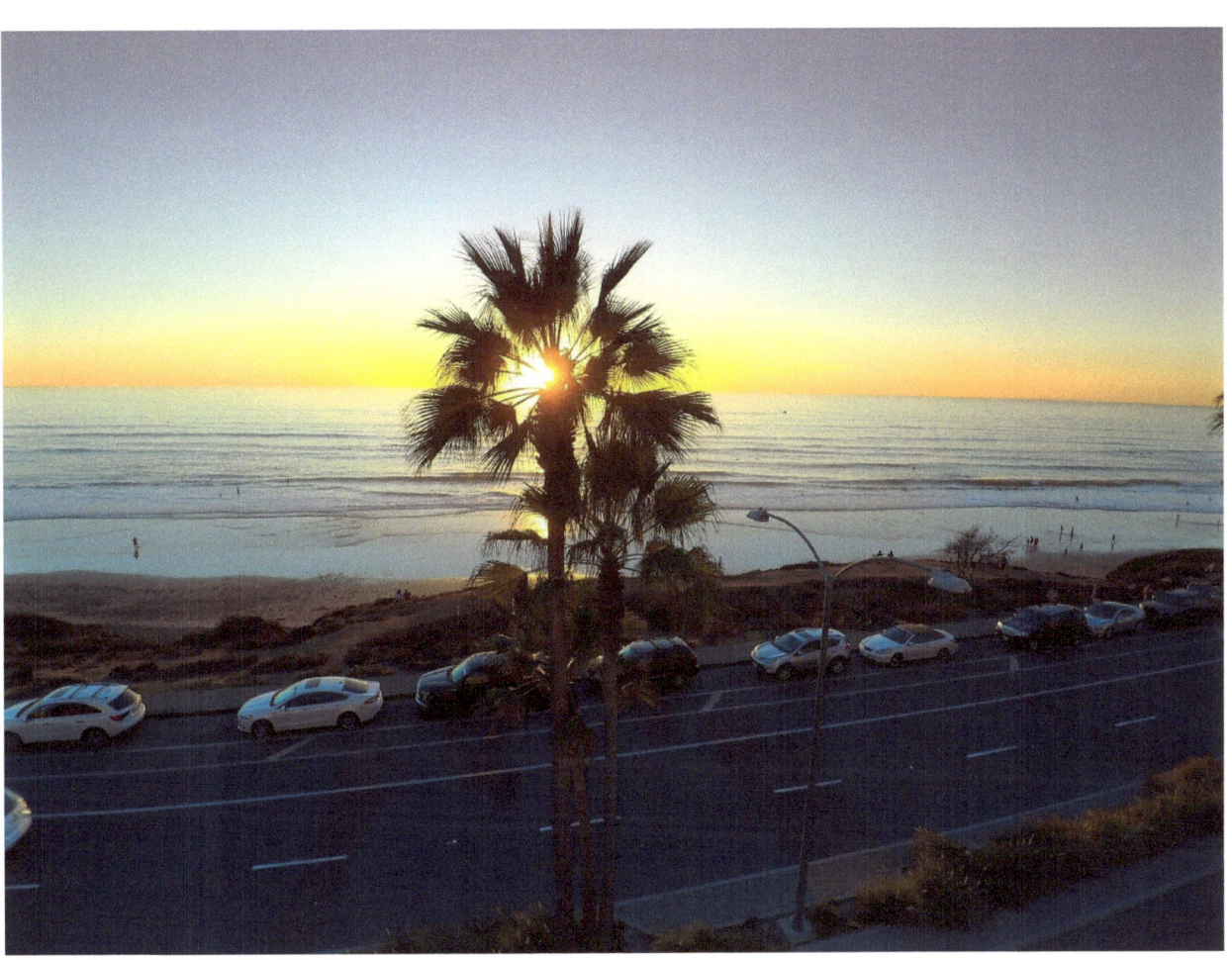

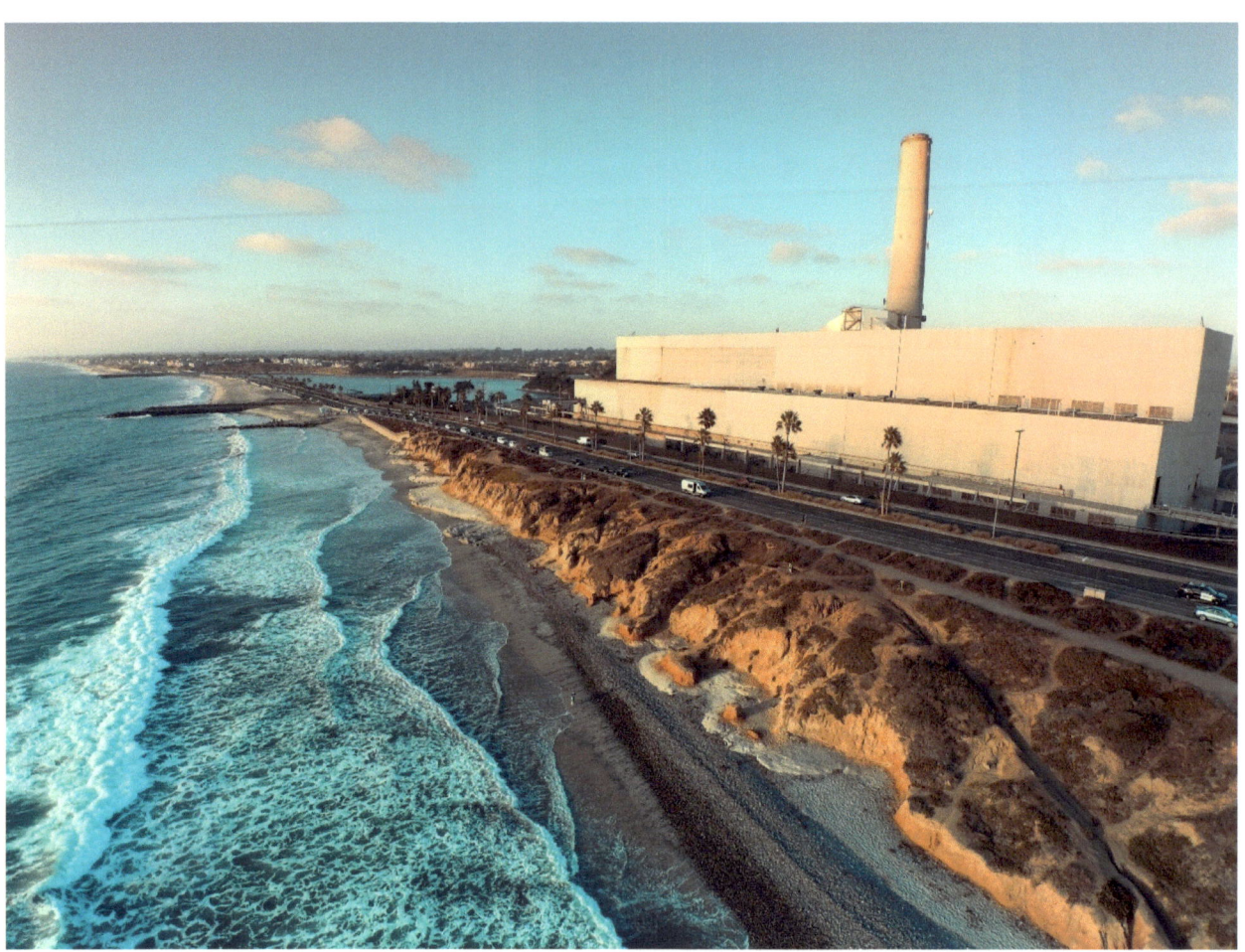

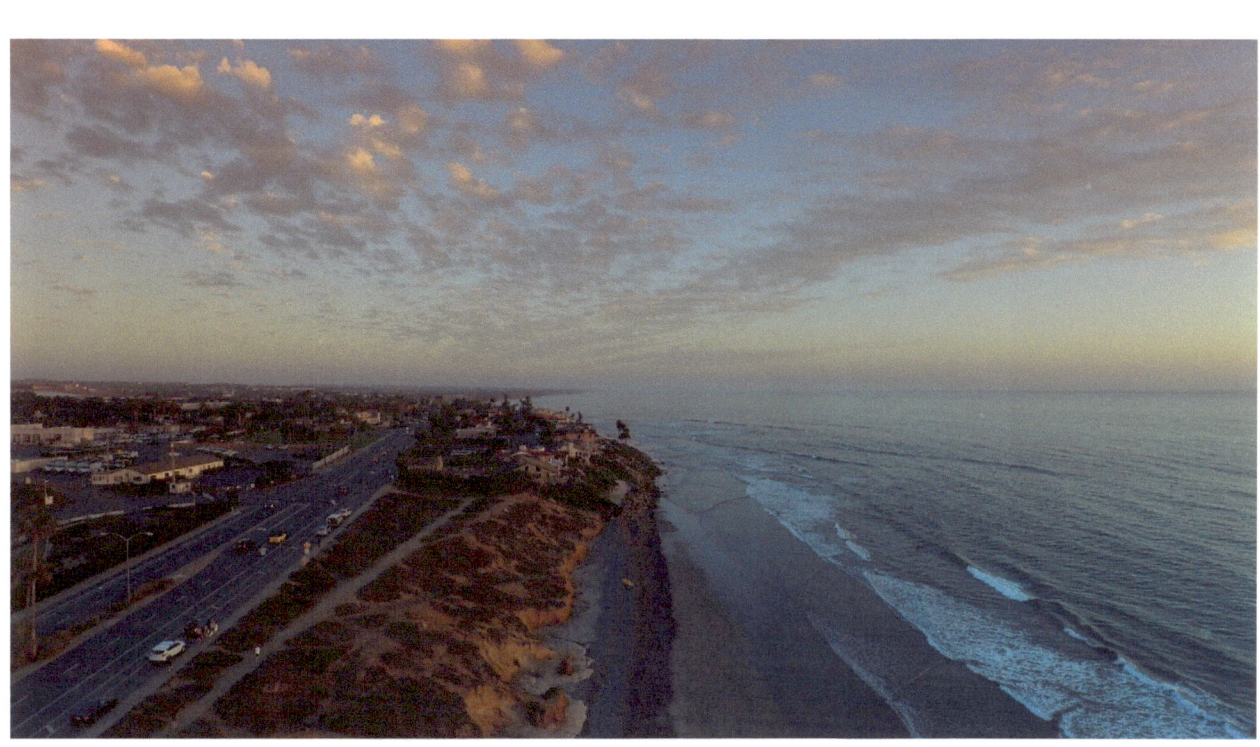

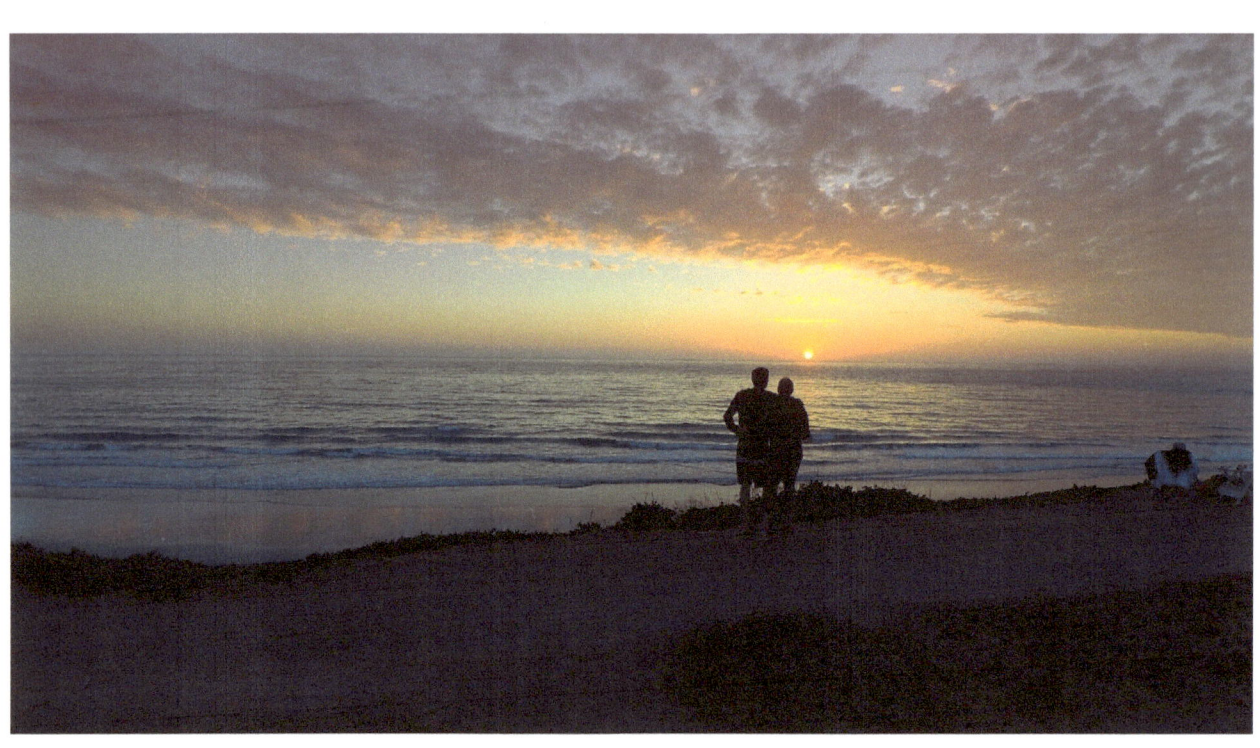

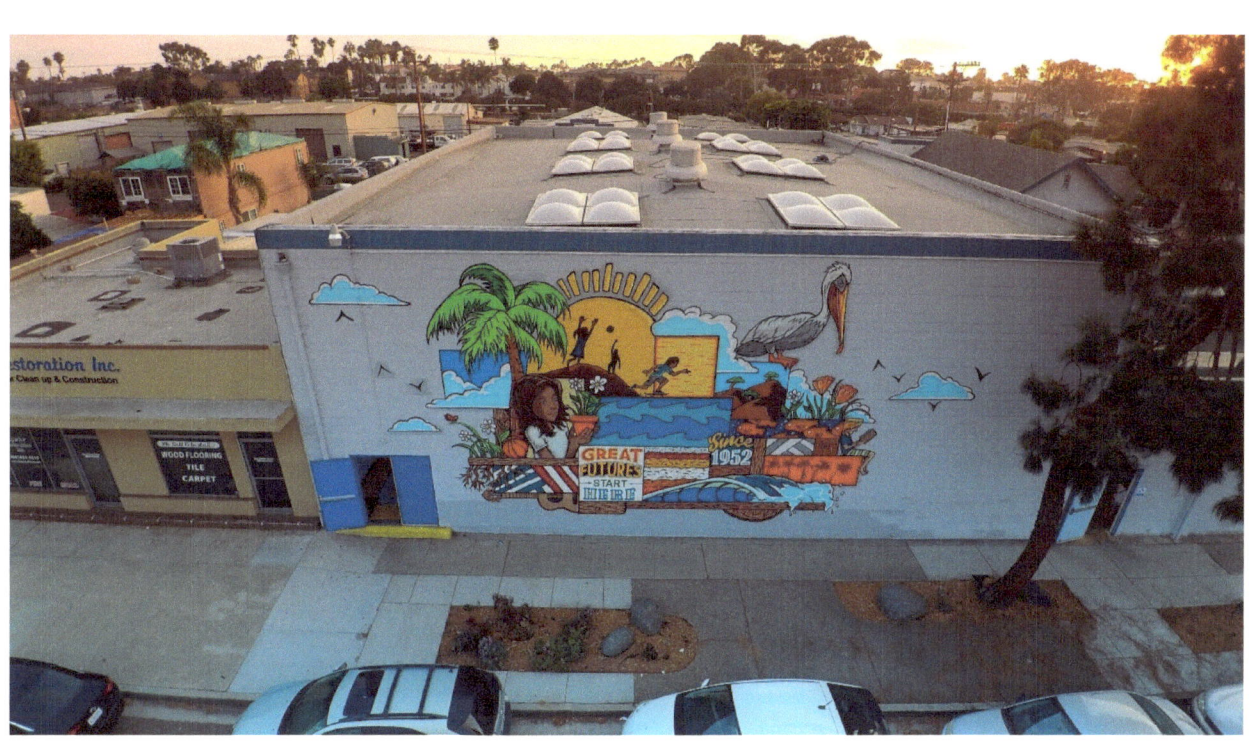

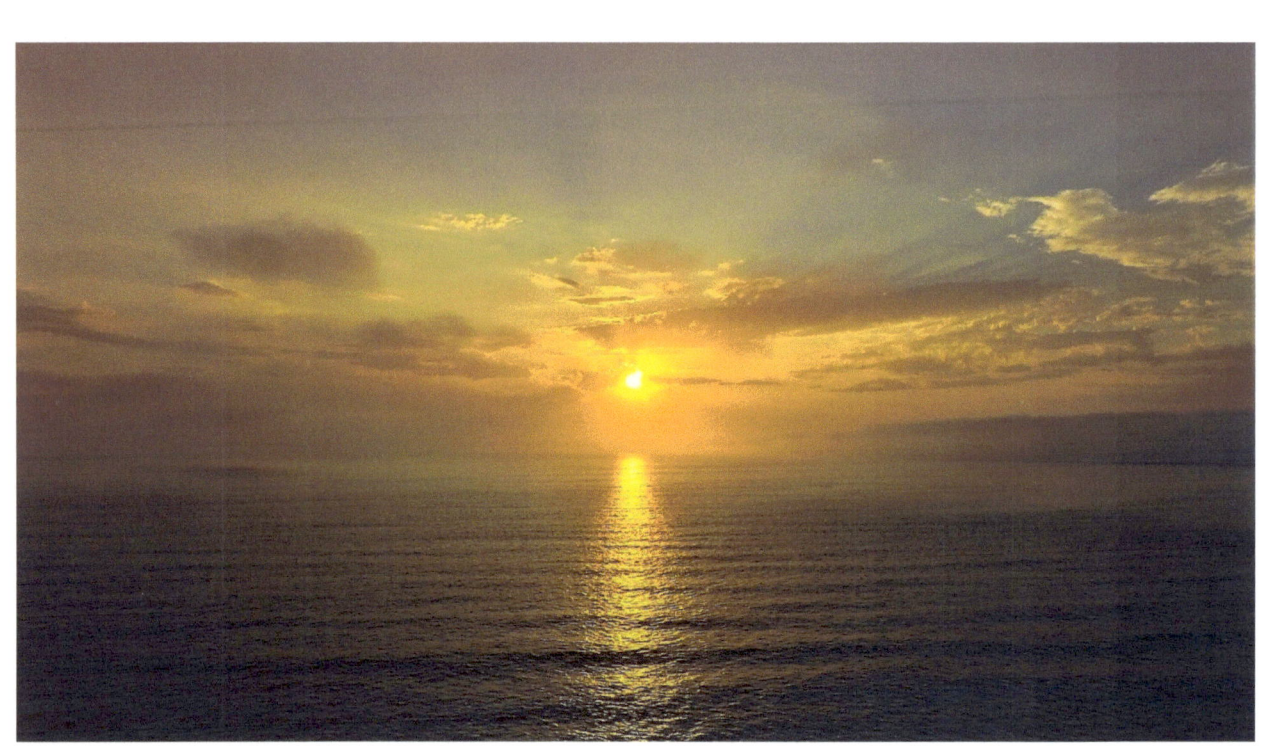

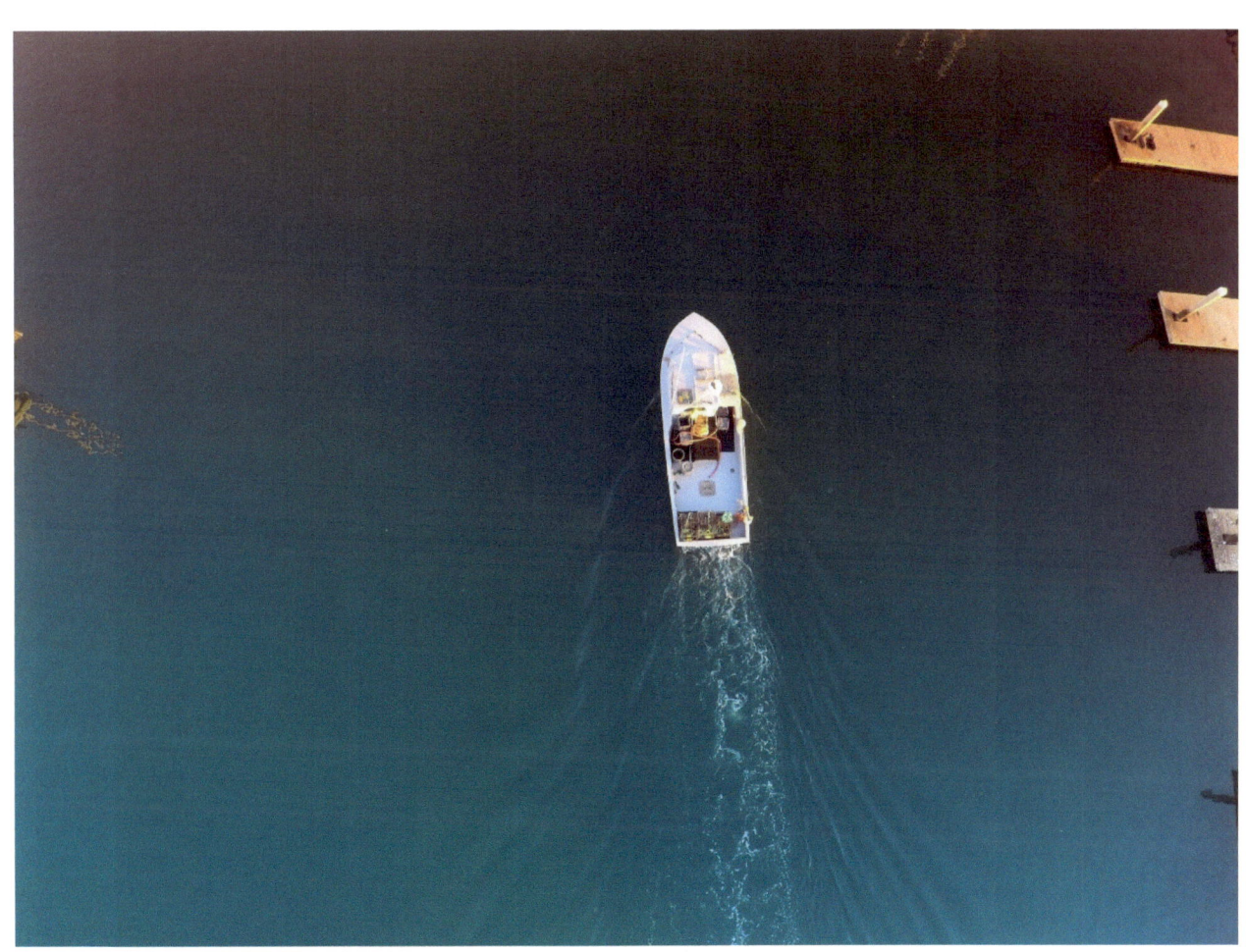

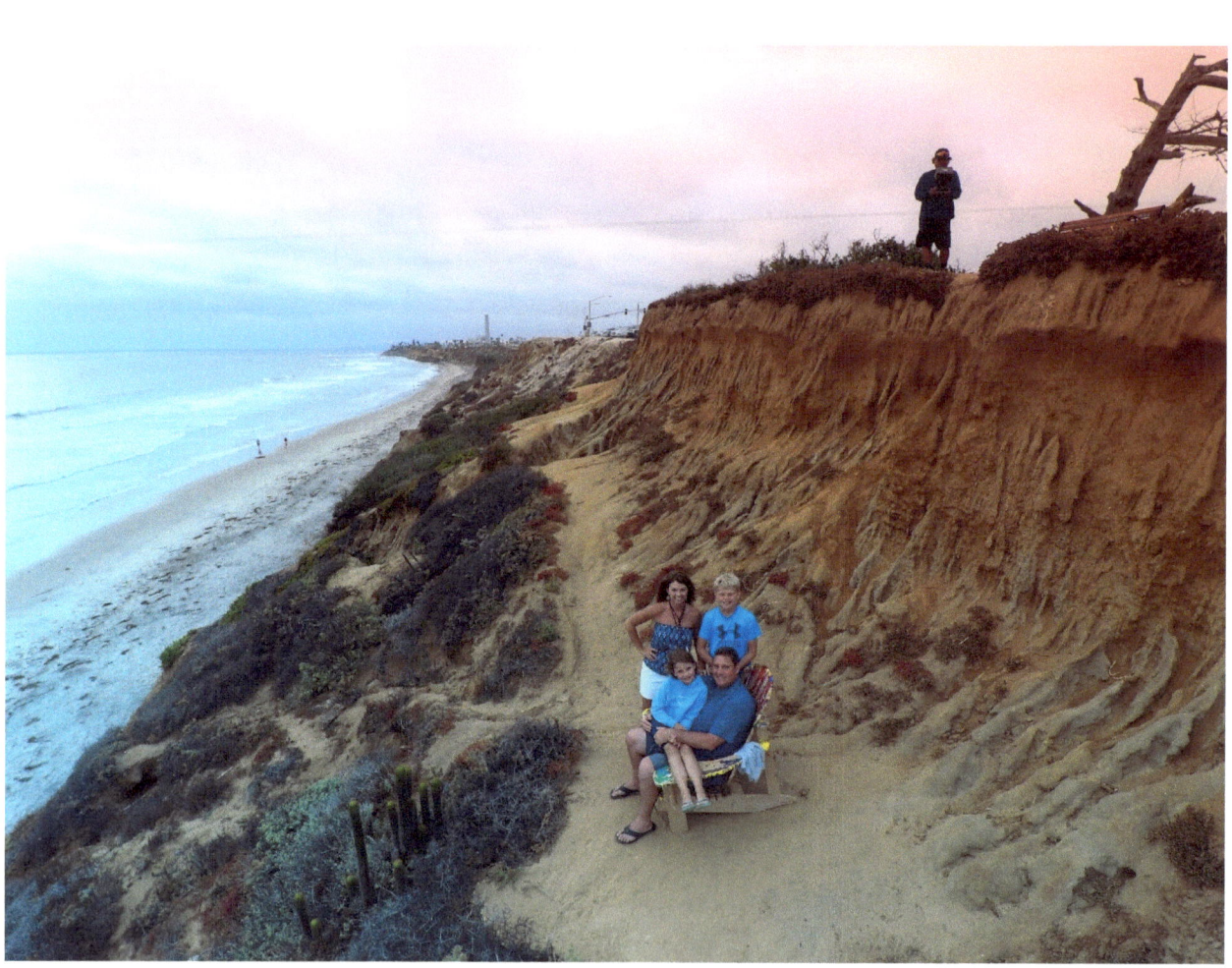

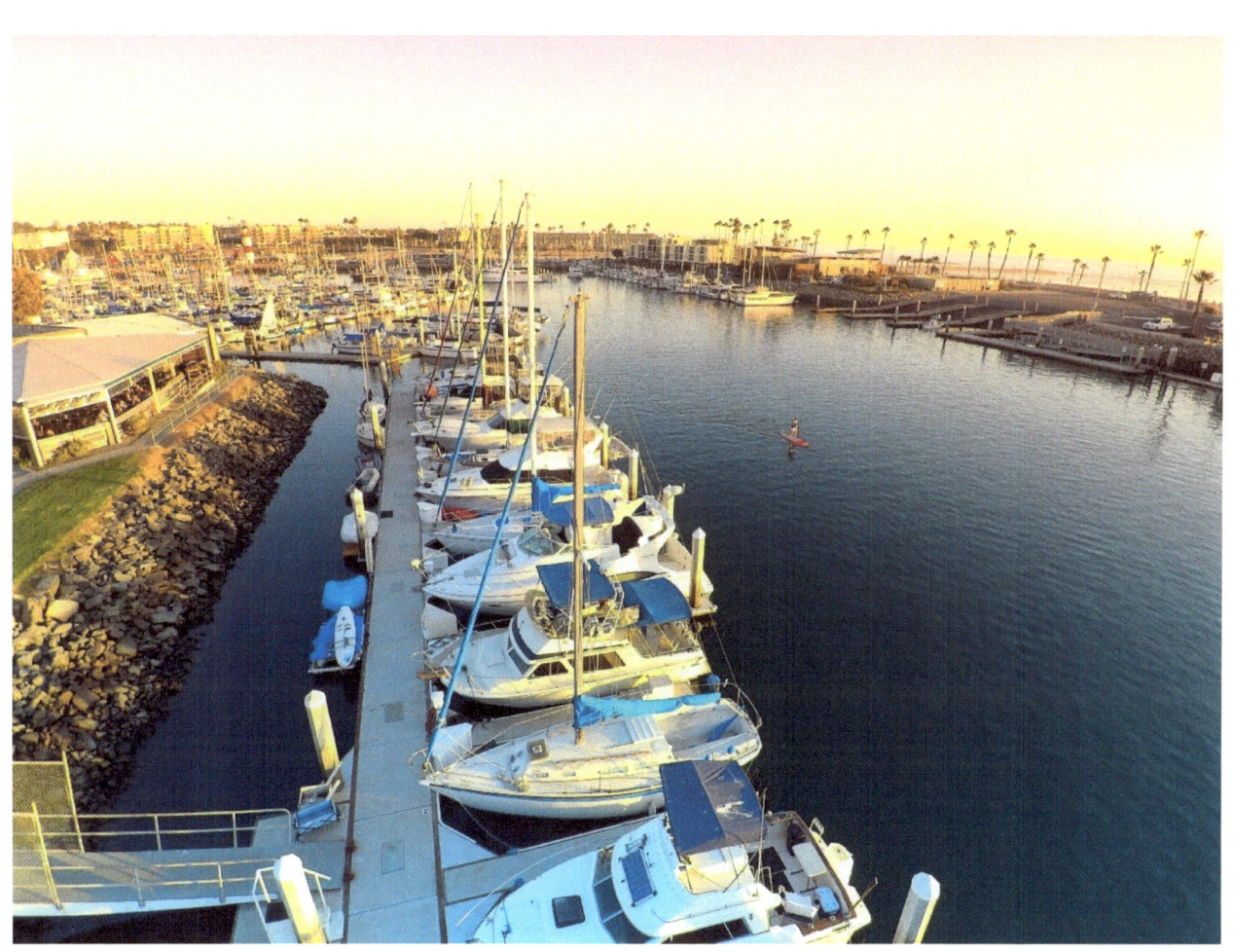

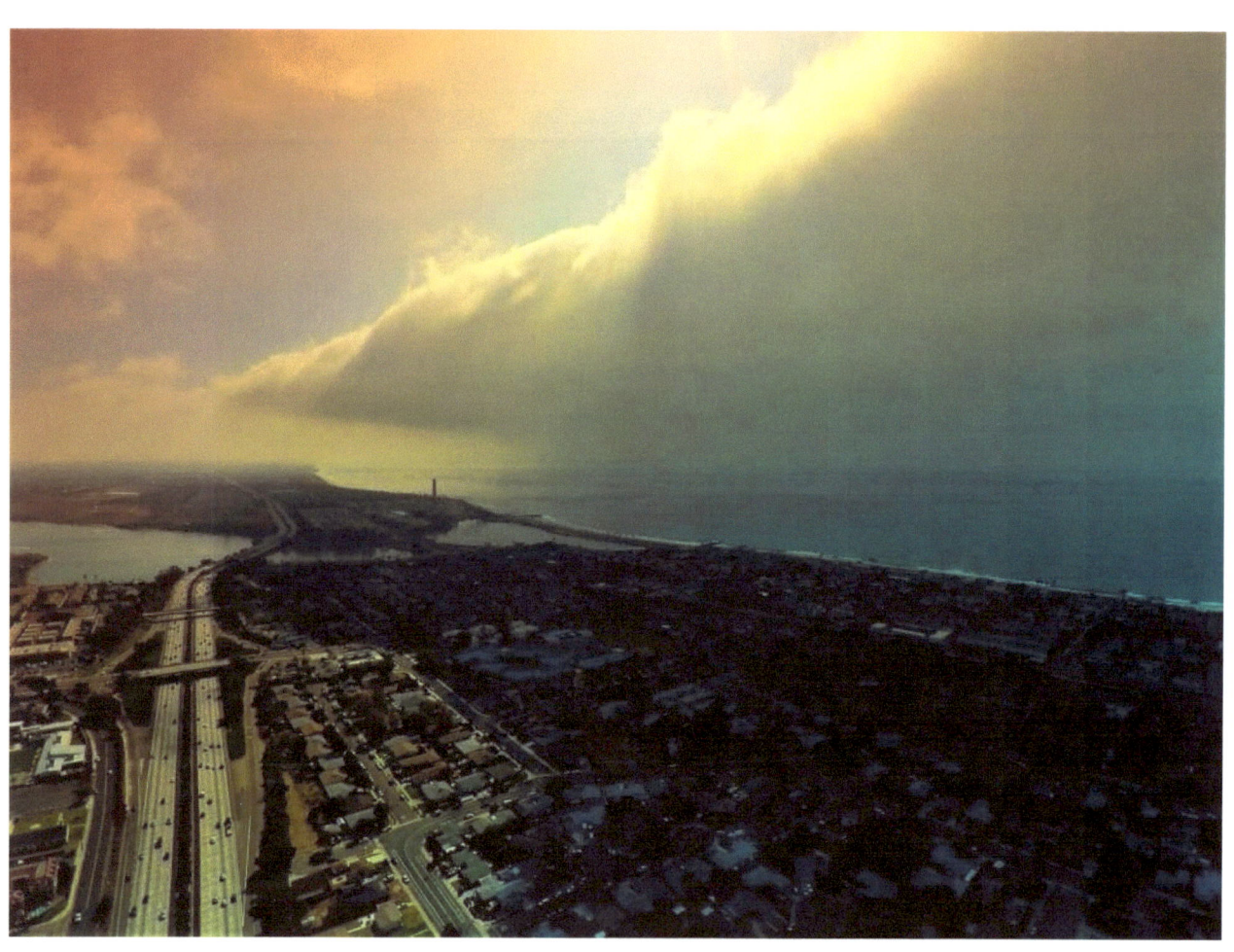

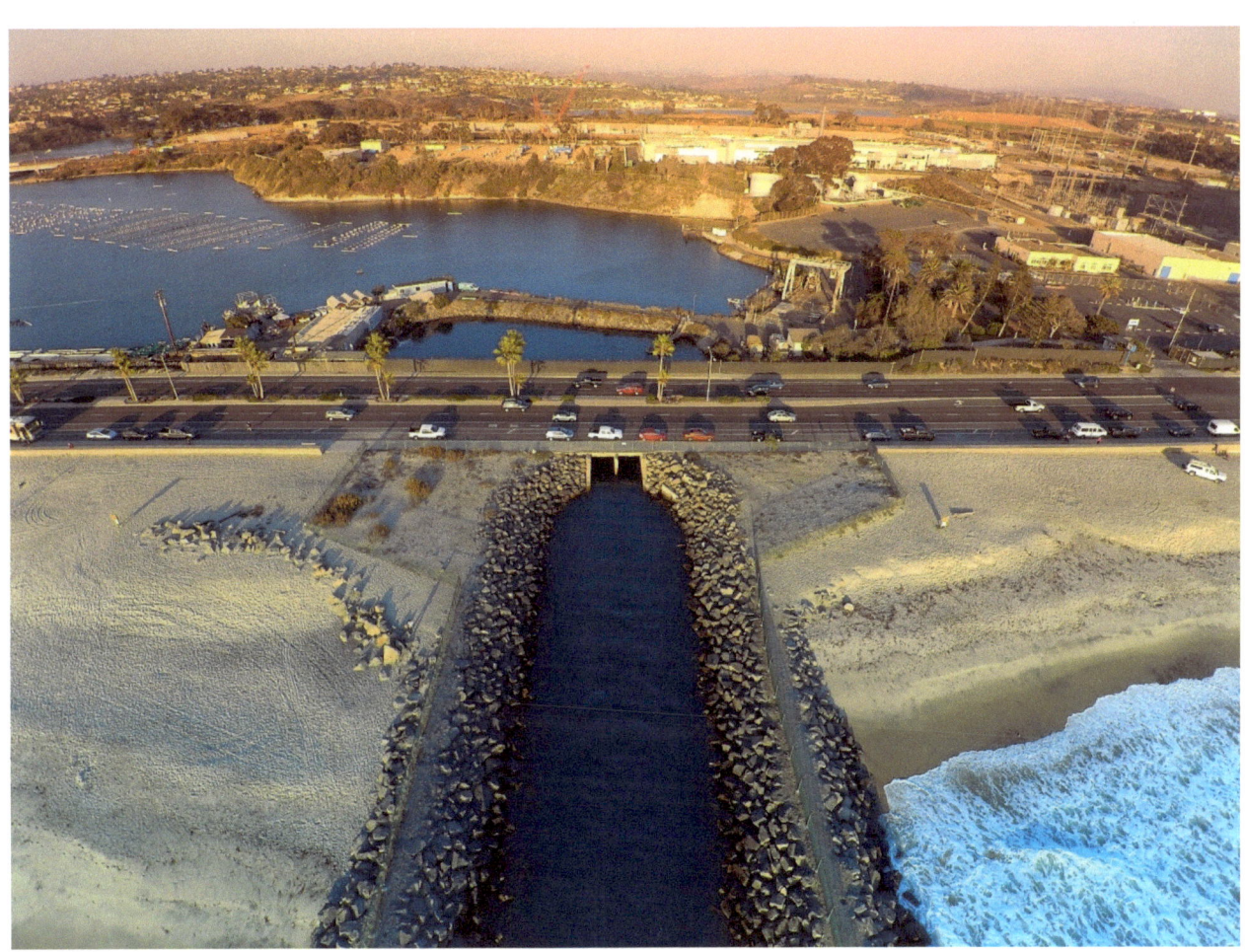

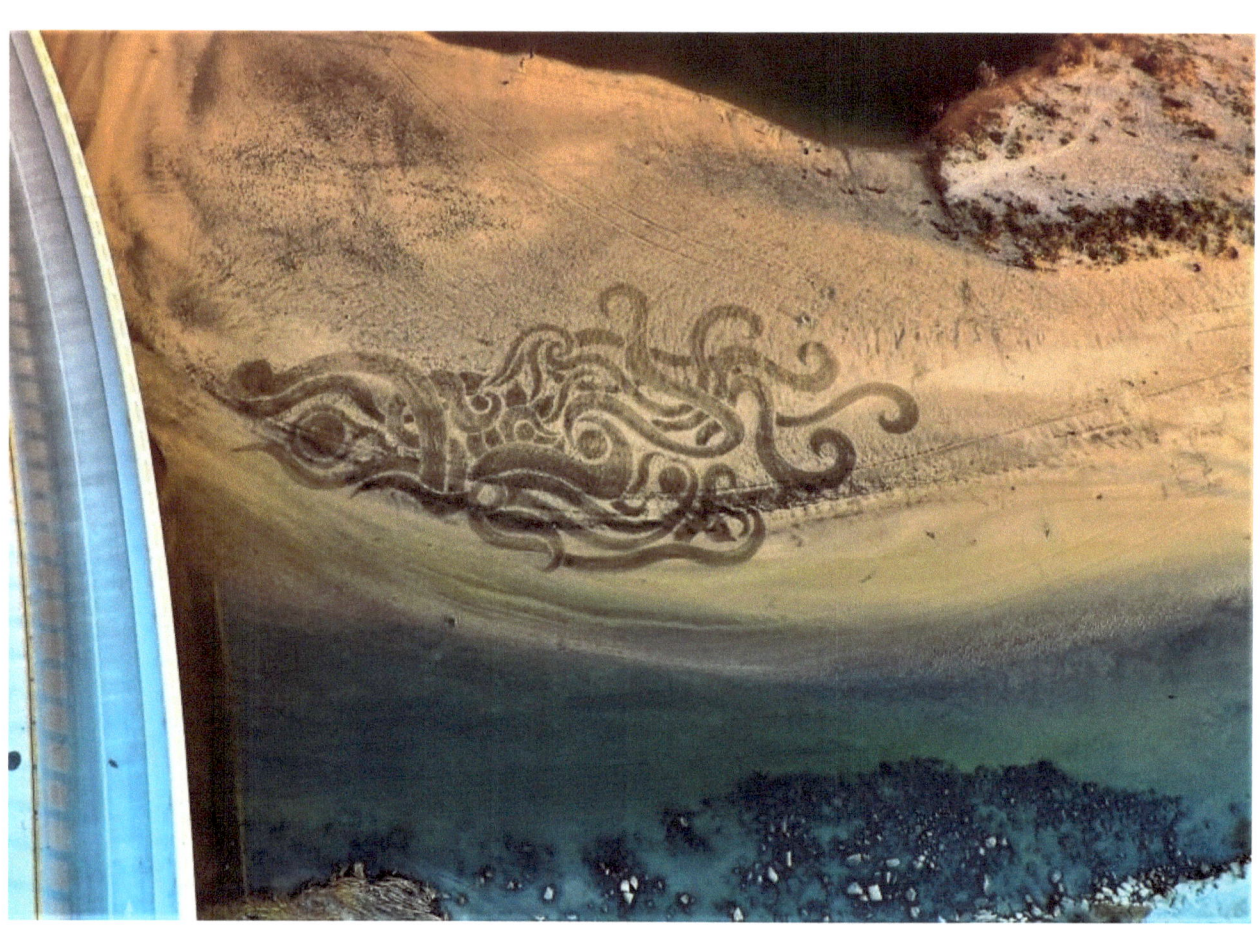

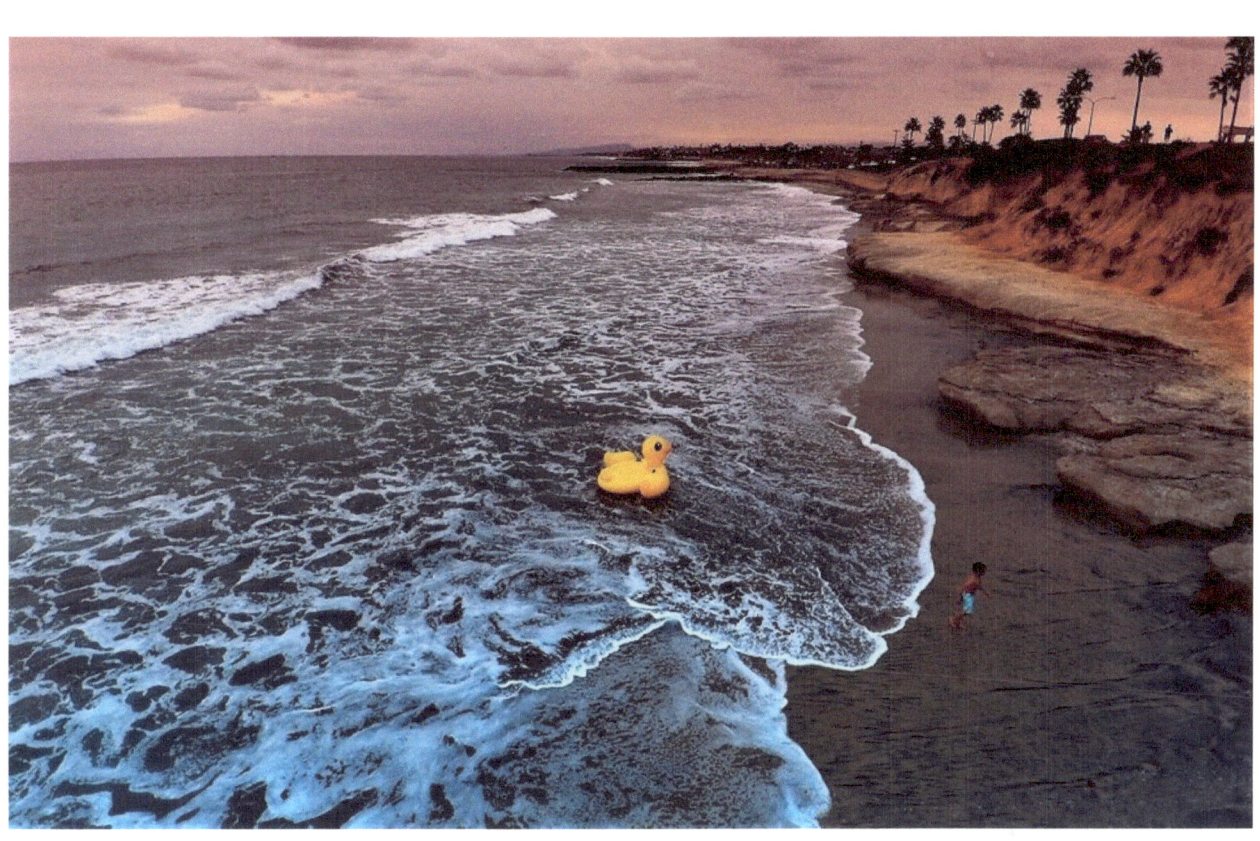

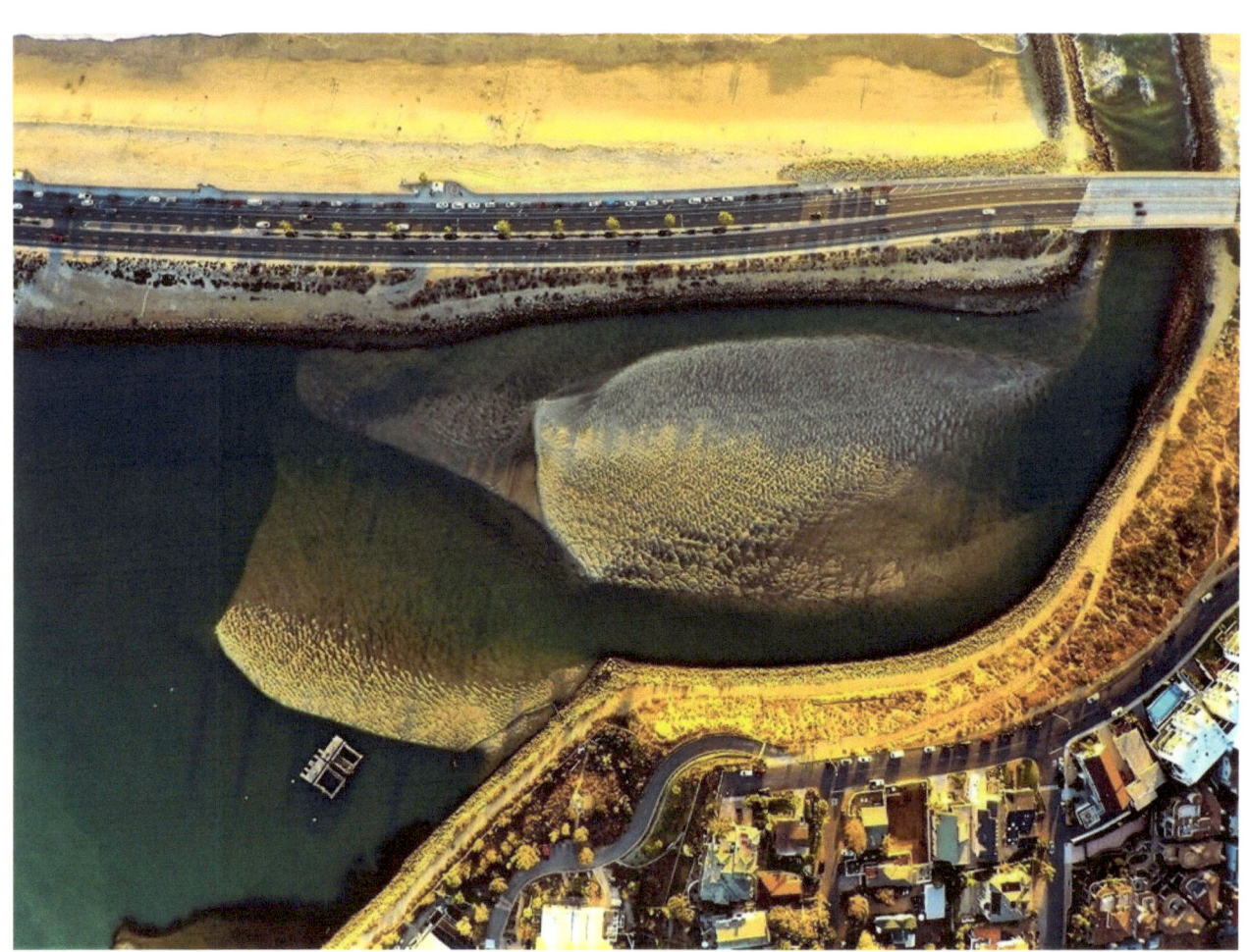

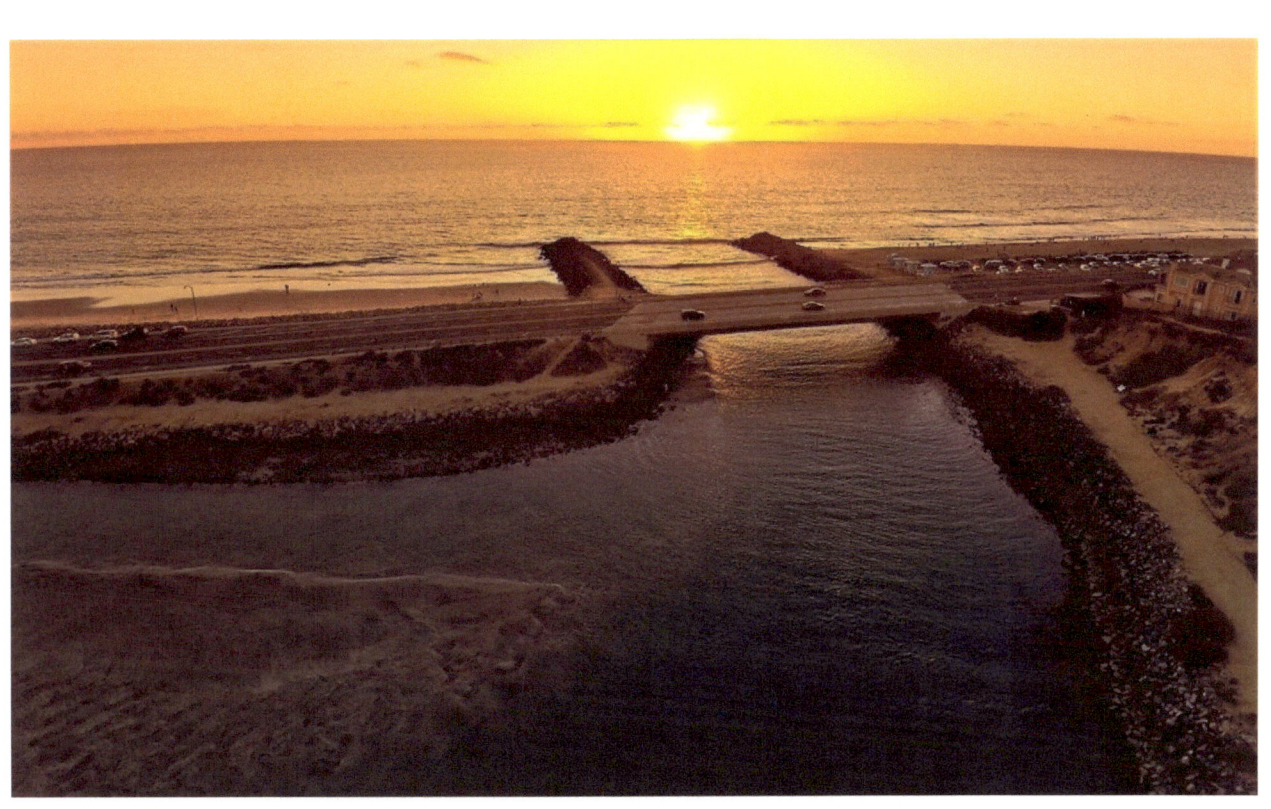

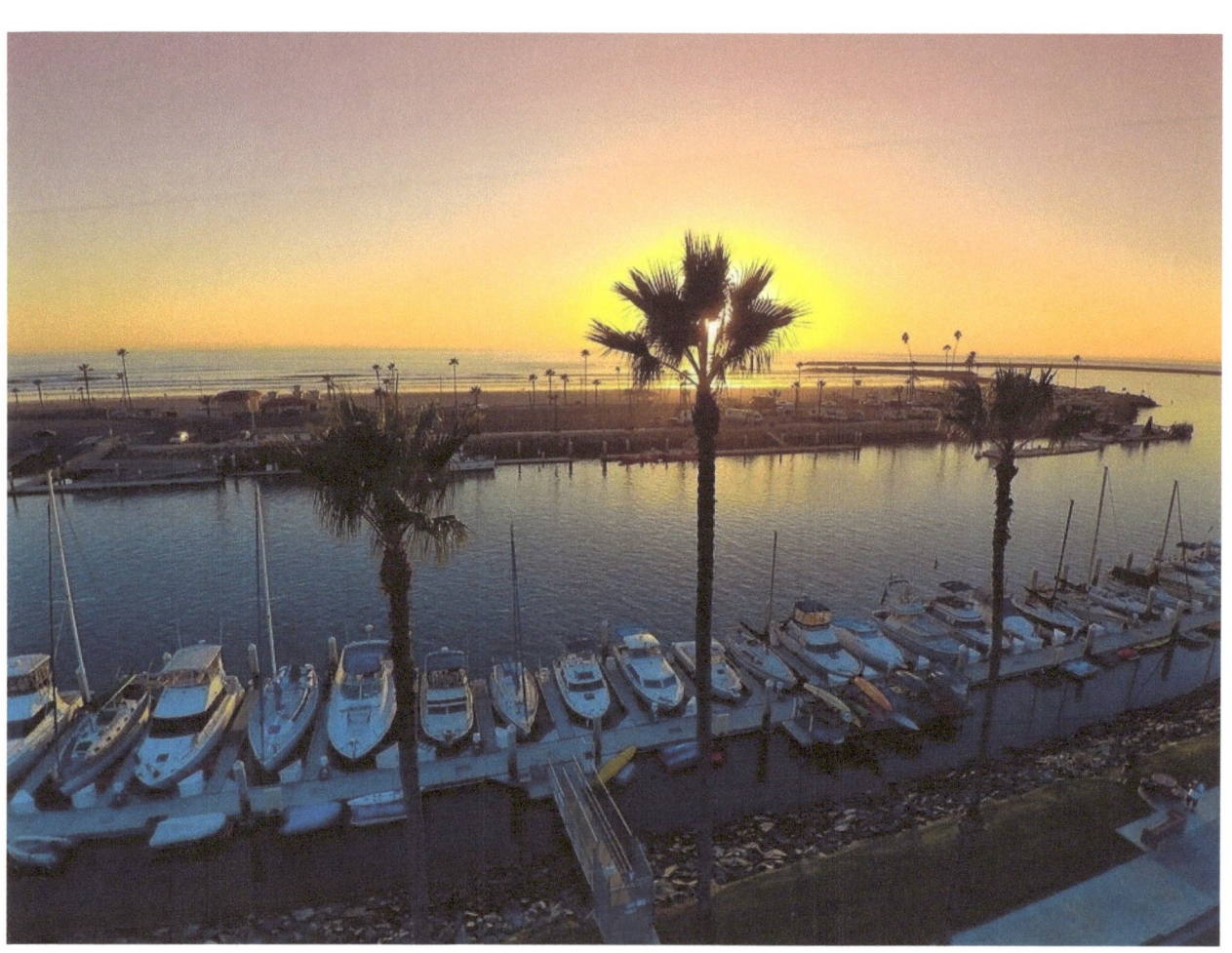

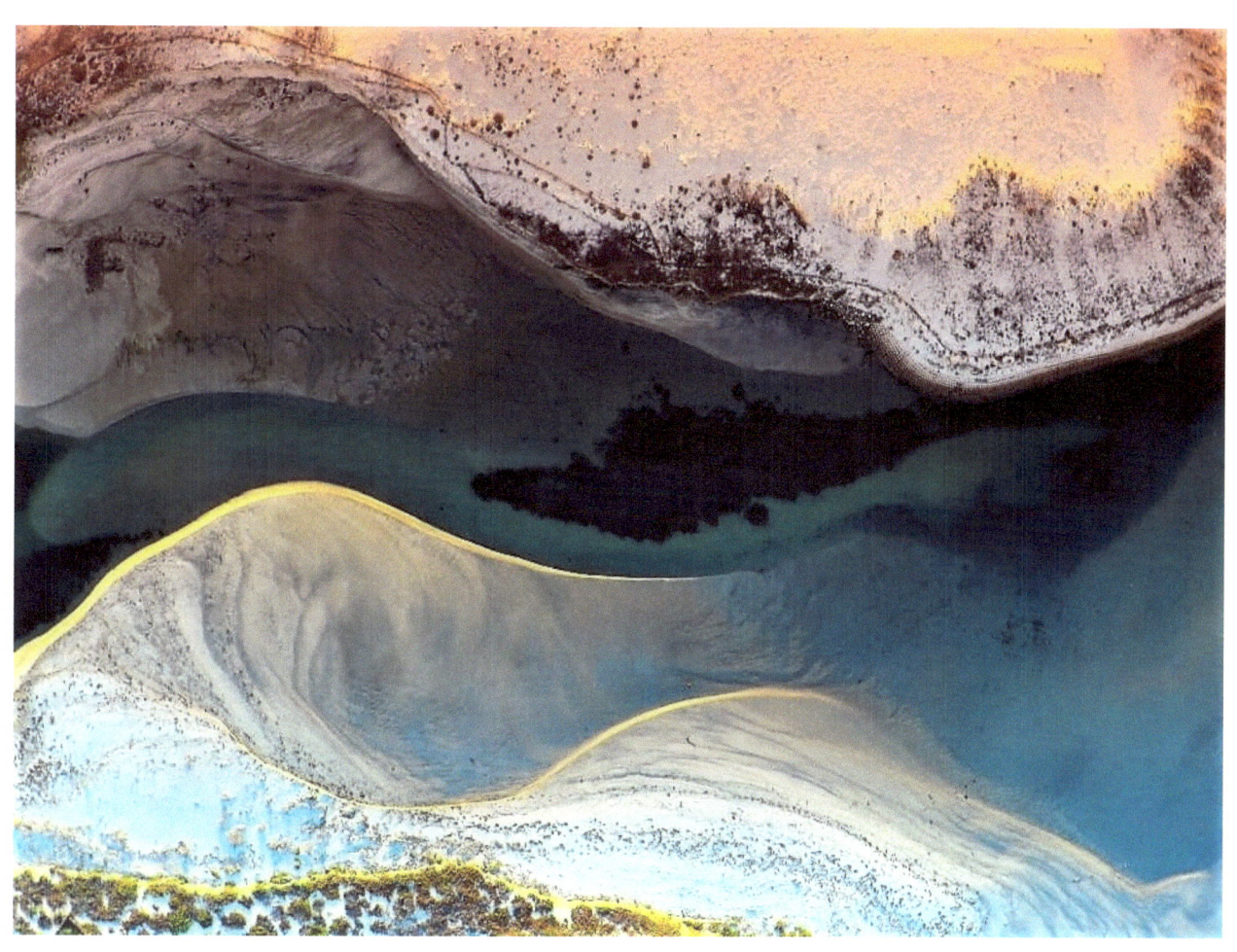

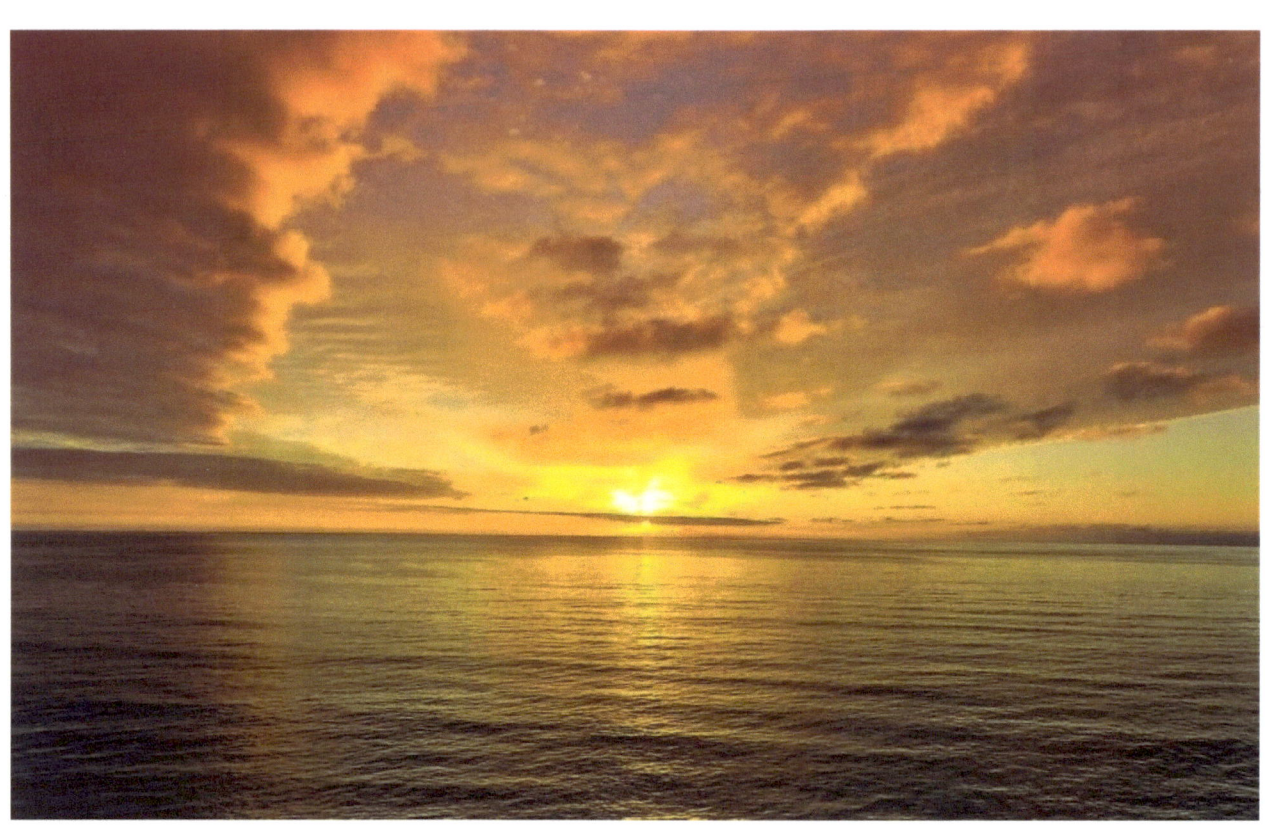

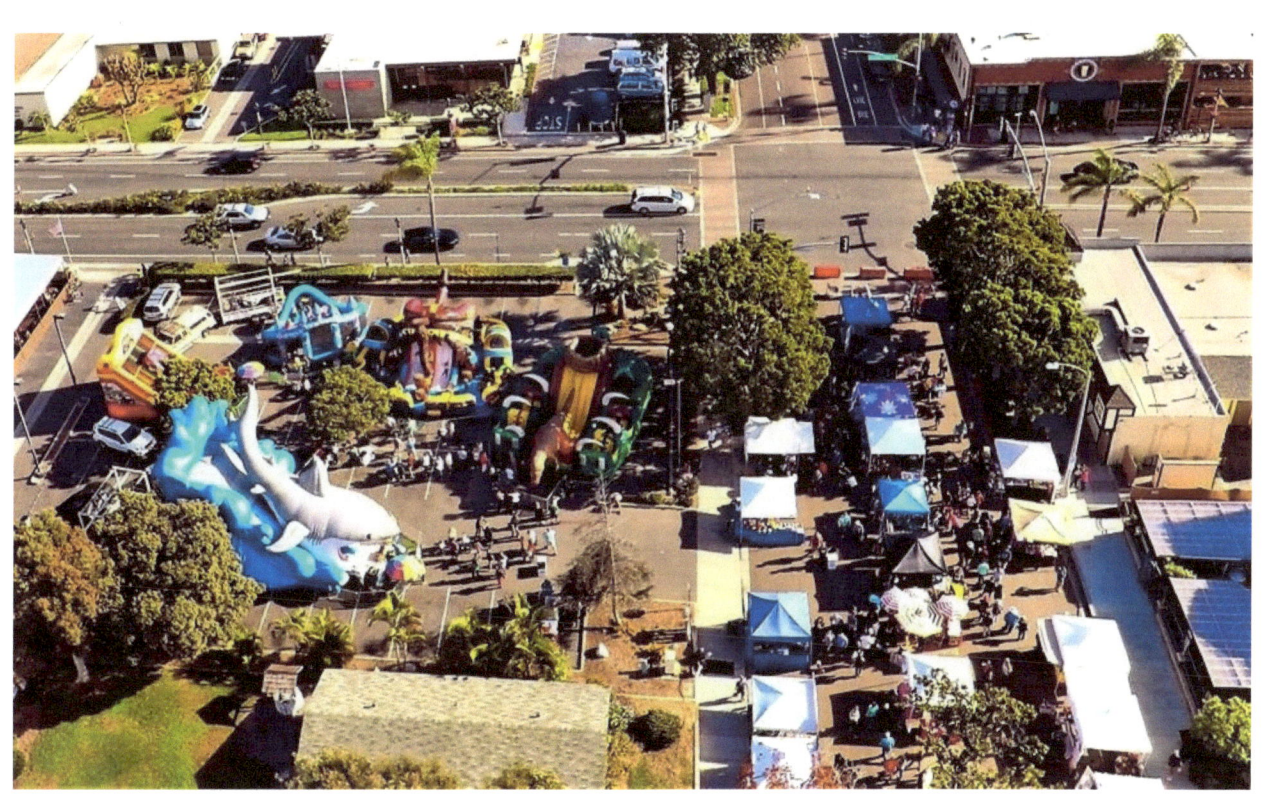

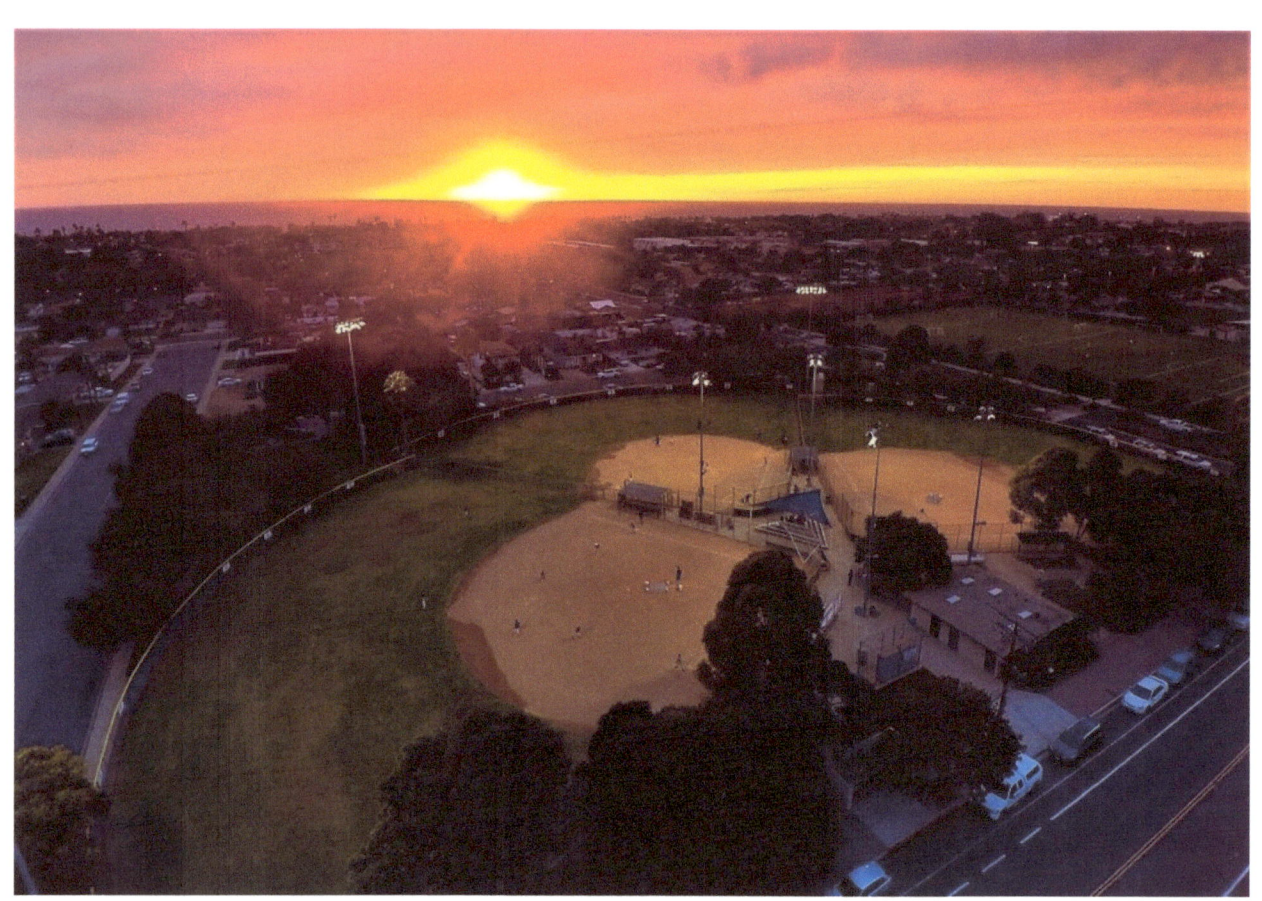

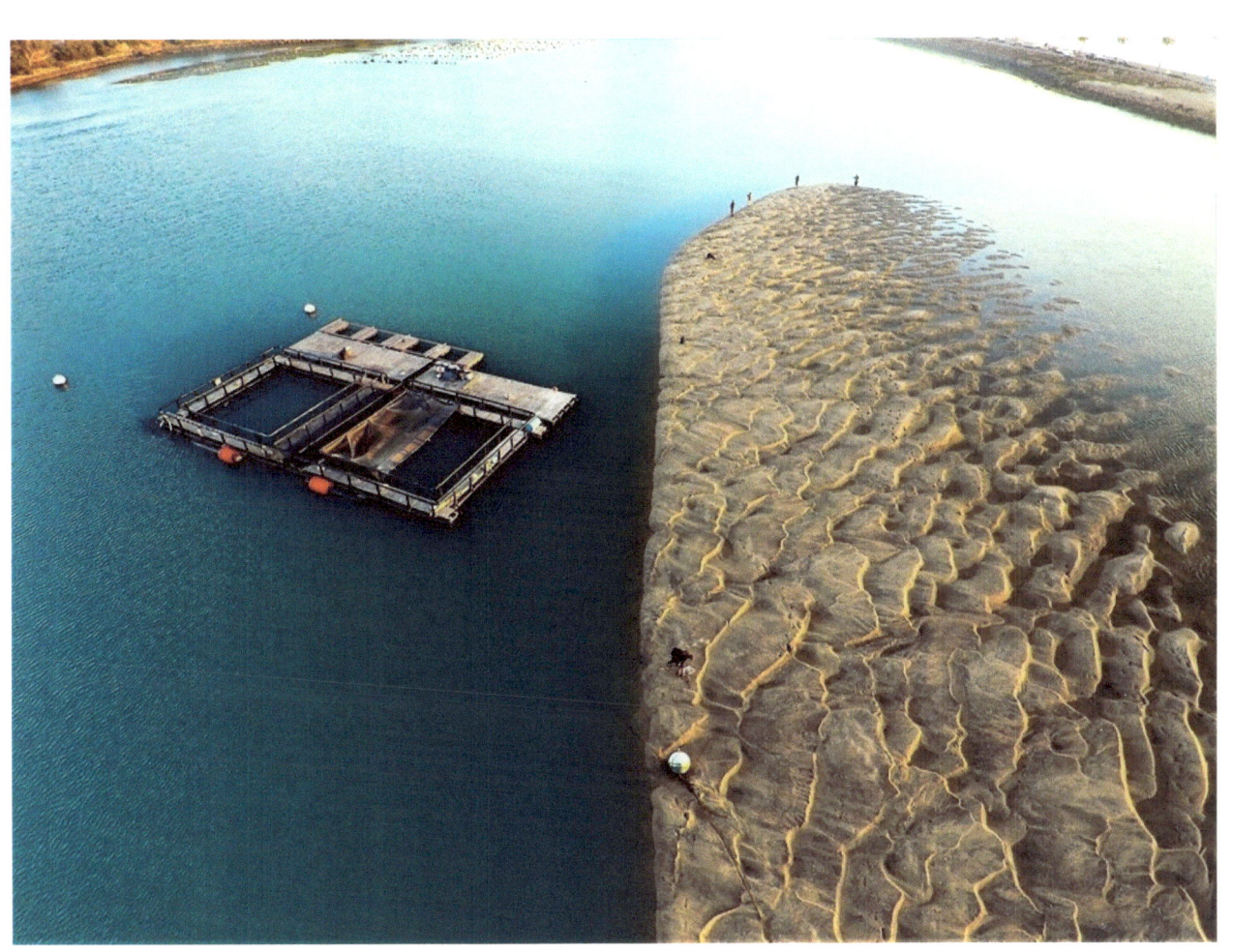

ABOUT THE AUTHOR

Born in Petaluma, California during the early 1970's, Bradley Zink grew up with a passion for books. Instilled in him by his parents, and surrounded with a library of books by Dr. Seuss, Mark Twain and Charles Dickens, to name a few, he developed a true passion for reading. After the birth of his son, Alex, and being a stay-at-home dad, he too instilled the power of reading in his son, too. Using Dr. Seuss as the building blocks for teaching him, Bradley aspired to create a book for Alex, and all children to enjoy. With his son as his muse and inspiration, Bradley is constantly testing out his writings on the world's harshest critic, his son Alex.

www.ingramcontent.com/pod-product-compliance
Lightning Source LLC
Chambersburg PA
CBHW040418220526
45473CB00004B/1281